21st CENTURY POSITIONING

PROVEN SELLING PRECEPTS

Jack Kinder, Jr. & Garry D. Kinder

TAYLOR PUBLISHING COMPANY - DALLAS

21st CENTURY POSITIONING
ISBN 0-9652791-9-7 $25
Cover Design by The Gray Group
Printed in the USA by Taylor Publishing

To order this title by mail, please send $25 plus $5 for shipping and handling. For each additional book ordered, add $2 shipping and handling. Send to: Kinder Brothers and Associates, Inc., 17110 N. Dallas Parkway, Suite 220, Dallas, TX 75248.

Or call toll-free 1-800-372-7110 to order using Visa, MasterCard or American Express -or for further information on books, sales support materials, consulting and speaking engagements from Kinder Brothers and Associates, Inc.

Library of Congress Cataloging-in-Publication Data

Jack, Garry
21st Century Positioning / by Jack and Garry Kinder

Includes index.
1. Creative ability in business. 2. Organizational change.
3. Corporate culture.
4. Success in business. I. Kinder, Jack and Garry

Dedication

This book is dedicated to the professionals who have discovered how to stay at their best through serving others. All we have learned from them we share with you.

"I don't know what your destiny will be, but one thing I know. The only ones among you who will be fulfilled and happy will be those who have sought and found how to serve others."

Dr. Albert Schweitzer

Acknowledgements

Thousands of you have contributed directly and indirectly to the development of the precepts identified in this book. To thank only a few may do a disservice to many. However, we are indebted to our colleague and partner at Financial Services Online, Joan Barrett, for her editorial assistance and helpful suggestions.

We are especially indebted to our personal assistants, Susan Newton and Cynthia Kerr. Susan typed, changed and typed again the manuscript. Cynthia contributed her proofreading skills to make the final product a superior one.

Thanks to Craig Clement and Gil Lozano for handling the many translations and for their marketing assistance.

Dr. Polly Cooper, the effective psychologist and teacher, commented very helpfully on the manscript format.

Finally, we could not have found a better graphics art team than Veo and Jo Gray of The Gray Group. Thanks to them for their design of the book jacket.

Contents

Section Three   **Selling Skill Developers**

Your Task

"Your task is to build a better world," said God;
   And I answered, "But how?
The world is such a vast place,
   And oh so complicated now.
I'm small and helpless,
   There is nothing much I can do."
But God in all His wisdom said,
 "Just build a better you!"

Foreword

21st Century Positioning is written for the dedicated few. *Success is almost always earned by the minority — the dedicated few who are willing to pay the price.*

Success begins with thoughts. Thoughts control our actions. Actions all too soon become habits. Habits shape and mold lives. This is one of the great psychological discoveries of the 20th Century. Our colleague of years past, Earl Nightingale, labeled it, *The Strangest Secret — "You become what you think about most of the time."* Actually, thousands of years earlier Solomon pointed out: *"Be careful how you think; your life is shaped by your thoughts."*

It is our belief that the best way to predict your future in selling is to create it. We believe you create a future, characterized by high performance and fulfillment, by making a responsible commitment to form sound habits of thinking, working, selling, studying and living right. We will feel well compensated for our efforts if the information and ideas developed on these pages motivate you to make this kind of commitment.

Professionals in selling display a blend of pro-active behaviors, enthusiasm and persistence. *They make commitments to excellence in all they do.* They resolve to make good on these commitments. Professionals know this requires maintaining a correct mental attitude, a good work ethic, sharpening persuasion skills, developing competence and living their lives in balance.

Successful salespeople are all-important catalysts for the free enterprise system. They have given America the highest standard of living in the world. They are individuals who deliver ideas and services to the consumer. They are goodwill ambassadors for their companies. They assist prospects in solving needs and problems through the utilization of their companies' products and services.

Through their efforts, salespeople provide livelihoods for more people than any other group in our society. *It's been estimated that one salesperson hired, trained and retained provides 27 other jobs. As a reward for their efforts, successful salespeople enjoy high standards of living.*

Salespeople who make responsible commitments to excellence are vital to our society. It is for this reason we have written this book, designed to provide inspiration and guidance to the men and women of this country who provide the fuel for the free enterprise system.

We've spent the past 20 years consulting, counseling and selling other professionals on doing better and being better. Our years of experience have taught us many things. It's our aim to share with you a rich storehouse of philosophies, principles and procedures that have enriched our lives and the lives of others.

As the incomparable Dr. O.S. Hawkins says: *"Being always comes before the doing. If you desire to do something great, you must first become something great."*

This is the theme that runs throughout this book. It's a theme we hope will position you for unusual selling success as you move to the 21st Century. Good luck and good selling,

Jack Kinder, Jr. - Garry D. Kinder

Section One
Attitude Conditioners

*In selling, we achieve to the degree that we condition
our attitude to stay positive. Overcoming the negative
is the price of achievement — the price of greatness.*

*Our attitude is not determined by circumstances, but by
how we respond to circumstances. Our minds determine
our attitude. We decide to respond positively or negatively.
It's how we react to events, not the events
themselves, that determines our attitude.*

Shape Your Future

Develop your own vision.
Define your dreams.
Set your goals.
Work out your action plan.
Develop the right habits.
Then just do it!

-Dexter R. Yager, Sr.

William Arthur Ward once wrote: *"Life is not so much a fight to be fought, a game to be played or a prize to be won. It's more nearly a work to be done and a legacy to be left."*

Self-assessment is the most important discipline you can employ to maximize your investment of time and money in reading this book. The Positioning Precepts we develop on these pages will be helpful to you only to the extent you "come to grips" with the major decisions in your life. We judge these major decisions to be the following:

1)   **What is your passion — long range?**
      Have you written out your Personal Mission Statement?

2)   **Are you excited about what you're doing?**
      How are you feeling about your progress and future?

3)   **Are you satisfied with what you're becoming?**
      Are you living the balanced life?

4)   **How do you plan to achieve financial security?**
      How much money will you need?

5)   **Are you contributing to the well-being of a larger community?**
      How will you achieve significance as well as success?

6) **Where will you get your motivation?**
What mentors and models will you have?

7) **When your epitaph is written, how will you want it to read?**
How do you want to be remembered?

Your responses to these issues will affect your 21st Century position in selling to a far greater degree than any other decisions you'll make personally or professionally.

Carlyle said: *"One life. Just a little gleam of time between two vast eternities. No second chance for us forevermore!"* We believe that's reason enough to shape your future, to plan and position yourself as a top performer for the 21st Century.
Dean Wm. T. Beadles, our renowned college professor, helped us discover the power of "moving the calendar" ahead five years — just 60 short months. Ask yourself this question: "During this time frame, what specific achievements must I produce so I will feel good about myself and my progress?"

Leaders in all walks of life are forward looking. They have a clear sense of where they are and where they are committed to go. Salespeople who reach the top rungs get there by first assessing where they are. Then they follow conscientiously and continuously their plan for shaping their futures!

This type of strategy converts to responsible commitments. And making responsible commitments is the starting point for shaping your future in selling.

This is the beginning of a new day.
　　God has given me this day to use as I will.
I can waste it ... or use it for good, but
　　What I do today is important, because
I am exchanging a day of my life for it!
　　When tomorrow comes, this day will be gone forever,
Leaving in its place something that I have traded for it.
　　I want it to be gain and not loss;
Good and not evil;
　　Success and not failure;
In order that I shall not regret
　　The price that I have paid for it.

-Dr. Heartsill Wilson

Positioning Precept
Shape Your Future

Develop The Winning Feeling

See yourself winning. Your self-image has to be strong, positive and optimistic before you get to the top. Somewhere along the way, you have to start thinking of yourself as more than just another competitor. You have to see yourself as a winner!

-Dennis Conner

Developing the winning feeling is the first principle of professionalism in selling. Why? *Because confidence in yourself will create the same feeling in others. They will believe in you, trust you, and have confidence in what you tell them.* When you speak with authority, your attitude must demand respect for that authority.

Of course, self-confidence differs from arrogance or conceit. You gain no respect when you display an arrogant attitude that seems to say, "Obviously, I know more about this than you do. I'm the absolute authority. You would be foolish not to listen to me and act upon my suggestions."

Conversely, self-confidence is a poised attitude which makes the other individual feel that he or she is being led by an experienced authority - not being ordered around by an egotist. The arrogant salesperson leaves prospects with the feeling they are being pushed into a decision. On the other hand, the self-confident salesperson leaves the individual with the impression that he or she has been helped. The prospect has been shown the benefits a certain product or service can bring. *The prospect feels that the decision is his or her own. The self-confident salesperson shows the prospect advantages he or she might not otherwise see, and simply assists the prospect in making the right decision.*

A lack of confidence in the slightest degree soon becomes apparent in your speech and manner. *But even more damaging, it's quickly reflected by a similar lack of confidence on the part of those you want to influence and sell.*

Selling with the winning feeling, the true professional learns the difference between discouragement and disappointment. He or she is aware that occasional disappointments may delay the fulfillment of desired objectives. But the professional is never discouraged into thinking the objectives will not ultimately be attained.

So, what is confidence? Since it is so important to your success, stop to think about your answer to this question. You will probably answer something like this: "Confidence is mostly a feeling." If this is true, then obviously you must strive to obtain that winning feeling. But how? How do you develop the winning feeling of confidence?

William James put it this way, *"Feelings seem to follow actions, but in reality, feelings and actions go together. By regulating the action, which is under the more direct control of the will, you can indirectly regulate the feeling which is not."* In this statement, James has given us the principle key to building confidence.

To develop the feeling of winning, you must first act the actions of winners. The actions you consciously perform become the most important factor in developing any desired feeling.

Since feelings are so important in everything you do, you must understand and constantly apply the formula for establishing that winning feeling. Within every individual is a natural inner power or source of power. *The formula we give you will synchronize your thoughts, actions and feelings and will help you release and use this "inner power."* Its application will develop the most confident, effective "you" possible. The formula is this:

Positive Thought + Positive Action = Winning Feeling

All action starts with thought. The thought of the conscious mind directs action. The combination of thought-plus-action scores an impression in the subconscious mind far easier and far deeper than could thought or action alone. The thought, plus its related action, more readily opens the mind, enters and etches a lasting impression in the subconscious. These new impressions are then reflected back as guiding patterns, influencing and increasing your positive actions. In other words, you are forming a "habit" or a "mode of behavior" that will soon lead to the involuntary or automatic process of thought-plus-action. And this in turn creates a feeling of success. *In effect, you are building a permanent success consciousness.*

Here are seven simple keys that will help you — ways in which you can develop this all-important winning feeling. These seven keys will help you synchronize thought-plus-action to produce the desired feeling.

Key No. 1 - Build Your Appearance Appearance affects attitudes — yours as well as your prospect's. Be aware of your posture. *Project a professional presence.*

Key No. 2 - Act The Part While this has long been known by the most successful people in selling, it seems to have escaped the great majority. *Whatever it is that you would like to do better, act as though you are already good at it.* If you continue to "play this part" long enough, you will become more and more competent at what you do. Use your imagination in a positive manner. Decide to be and stay an optimist. Hang on the walls of your mind pictures of those things you desire to achieve. *See possibilities, not problems. See opportunities, not obstacles. Expect the best — and act the part.*

Key No. 3 - Speak Faster This seems like a rather simple instruction. To many, it's a new idea. *Make a habit of increasing your rate of speech and take note of its impact on others.* Immediately, you will appear and feel more enthusiastic and confident.

Key No. 4 - Compete, But Don't Compare You should compete with your friends and associates, but you should never compare. "Keeping up with the Joneses" adds unneeded pressures to your selling life. Build your own "game plan." *Compare your life with what you ought to be.*

Key No. 5 - Practice What You Do Well Confidence flows best from successful experiences. Build on your strengths.

Key No. 6 - Cooperate With Life Focus your attentions and energies on those things you can do something about.

Key No. 7 - Develop A Mentor Find someone who will be genuinely interested in your successes.

Follow these seven key instructions. You'll soon begin to perform with more confidence. This is the first step to greater productivity.

As with anything else, the best place to start is where you are right now. *Of one thing you can be certain — you'll never be sorry for taking command of your thinking and acting as it relates to winning in selling.* Put these action keys to work every day. Follow them until they become habits — until your selling style automatically assumes a position of confidence.

Positioning Precept
Develop The Winning Feeling

Bloom Where Planted

Be committed to bloom where you're planted.
Forming this habit breeds in you self-discipline,
imagination and staying-power.

-The Kinders

Each year thousands of young men and women enter the selling profession. Some make responsible commitments, develop their skills and go ahead to achieve unusual selling success. But far too many give this business of selling a timid, tentative try — never really getting themselves set up for success — and then turn to other fields.

In a way, they remind us of the farmer in the "Acres of Diamonds" story. Some stories are too powerful to grow old. "Acres of Diamonds" is one of them. No one knows who told it the first time. But the man who made it famous was Dr. Russell Herman Conwell. By telling the story all over America, Dr. Conwell raised millions of dollars with which he founded Temple University in Philadelphia. This fulfilled his lifetime dream to build a fine school for poor but deserving young people.

Dr. Conwell told the story "Acres of Diamonds" more than 6,000 times. He attracted great audiences wherever he appeared. The story is about a farmer who lived in Africa, at the time diamonds were discovered there. One day a friend told him of the millions being made by men who were discovering diamond mines. The farmer promptly sold his farm and left to search for diamonds himself.

He searched all over the continent. But he found no diamonds. And, as the story has it, finally penniless, in failing health and despondent, he threw himself into a river and drowned.

Long before this, the individual who had bought the farm found a large, unusual-looking stone in the creek bed which ran through the farm. He placed it on his mantel. Enter here the same visitor who had told the original farmer about the diamond discoveries. He examined the stone and told the new owner that he had discovered one of the largest diamonds ever found — and that it was worth a fortune. To his surprise, the farmer told him the entire farm was covered with stones of that kind.

The farm, which the first farmer had sold so that he could go look for diamonds, turned out to be one of the richest diamond mines in the world.

The point Dr. Conwell made was that the first farmer had owned acres of diamonds, but had made the mistake of not examining what he had before he ran off to something he hoped would prove to be better.

No matter where you live, what company you represent, or what product you sell, you are surrounded by acres of diamonds, if you'll simply stick and stay long enough to discover them. Like the curious-appearing stones which covered the farm, they might not appear to be diamonds at first glance, but with a little time and some polishing, they will reveal unusual opportunities. We know of no other profession where you can, in a short period of time, earn the kind of income enjoyed only by top strata corporate executives after years of experience.

Whatever we think we're looking for can usually be found right where we are, in the old familiar surroundings. That's what's wrong — *the surroundings are so familiar to us that we take them for granted as the first farmer did.* We overlook the acres of diamonds under our feet to look for them elsewhere.

Here are three philosophies relative to this subject which we have carried on 3x5 cards for years. We recommend you refer to them often and inwardly digest them.

"The people who get on in this world are the people who get up and look for the circumstances they want, and if they can't find them, make them." - George Bernard Shaw

"Nothing in the world can take the place of persistence. Talent will not; nothing is more common than unsuccessful people with talent. Genius will not; unrewarded genius is almost a proverb. Education will not; the world is full of educated derelicts. Persistence and determination alone are omnipotent." - Calvin Coolidge

"In most things, success depends on knowing how long it takes to succeed." - Montesquieu

For some, it may well be that greener pastures lie elsewhere and they should move on. But it's a good idea to prospect the ground we've got before we start looking someplace else.

Positioning Precept
Bloom Where Planted

Be A Peak Performer

*The first thing to do, if you have not done it, is to fall
in love with your work. Hold yourself responsible
for a higher standard than anybody else expects
of you. Never excuse yourself. Never pity
yourself. Be a hard taskmaster to yourself.*

-Henry Ward Beecher

Successful salespeople come in all shapes and sizes. They vary
widely in education, experience and occupational backgrounds.
However, those who manage to go to the top and stay there have
certain common denominators. We've discovered that Peak
Performers have these four characteristics in common:

1) **Peak Performers Pay Attention** - They don't just look,
   they see something. They don't just listen, they hear something.

2) **Peak Performers Pay the Price** - They have a passion to
   excel at what they do. No price is too great. They are fully
   committed to winning. Peak Performers focus. They consistently do the things their competitors will not or cannot do.

3) **Peak Performers Are Promoters** - They effectively work
   at becoming known for what they know. They are often
   referred to as opportunists. They are sensitive to ways in
   which they can distinguish themselves. They may do this
   by designing an attractive brochure, which includes endorsements. They may speak at a civic club or write an
   article for a trade publication. Peak Performers are contact-
   conscious.

4) **Peak Performers Persist** - They believe in the type of
   philosophy advanced by Cyrus Hall at Hallmark Cards.
   Hall said, *"When you reach the end of your rope, tie a knot
   and hang on!"*

To join the elite fraternity in sales referred to as Peak Performers, learn to pay attention, be motivated to pay the price, be effective at promoting yourself and persist.

Dexter Yager is respected throughout the sales world as one of its most influential Peak Performers. We read one time where Dexter attributed his excalibur peak performance to seven character builders. We've recommended these to our sales audiences and we strongly recommend them to you. These seven character-building tips are behavior changing.

- *Avoid the crybaby mentality.* Into each life some rain will fall. Expect it. Accept it. Forget it.
- *Fight fairness frustration.* It's those who make the most of the cards they are dealt who become Peak Performers.
- *Stop being a brooder reactor.* You will never do well if you tend to dwell.
- *Don't get down on yourself.* Compete but don't compare. Lean to the positive.
- *Don't depend on other people's approval.* People-pleasing can paralyze you into indecision.
- *Overcome personal cowardice.* Act courageously.
- *Let your career be ruled by God.* As Carlyle said, *"It's the spiritual that determines the material."*

Peak Performers embrace the Dexter Yager philosophies. They also believe in the great thought developed by Wilfred Peterson when he wrote these lines:

> *Do not work to make a living,*
> *Rather work to make a life.*
> *For the measure of succeeding*
> *Is your service in the strife.*
> *All you ever leave behind you,*
> *When your soul has crossed the bay,*
> *Is the good you've done for others.*
> *You must go, but it will stay!*

Positioning Precept
Be A Peak Performer

Visualize Desired Outcomes

I try to picture a ride in my mind before I get on the bull.
Then I try to go by the picture.

-Larry Mahan

Dr. Carl Sorensen, a professor at Stanford University, says it well, *"There's an old expression, 'Seeing is believing.' But it is more accurate to say that 'believing is seeing.' That is, you tend to see what you believe you're going to see. You bring to a situation what you expect you're going to experience."*

Your mind talks to your body by using mental images. This dialogue is going on all the time. *Your mind may think in words, but your body responds to images as though they were actually happening right now.*

Many professional athletes find visualization to be a powerful tool to enhance their performance. As baseball legend Yogi Berra once said, *"Ninety percent of the game is mental, and the other half is physical."*

The colorful Mary Lou Retton was the first American woman to win an individual gold medal in gymnastics. In an interview with *The Mind-Body Health Digest,* she said, *"Doing mental imagery was always a constant for me. I'd see myself performing in my head, and it really helped tremendously. It gave me confidence."*

Jerry Rice, all-pro wide receiver of the San Francisco 49ers, caught 11 passes for a record-shattering 215 yards in the 1989 Super Bowl and caught a record three touchdown passes in the 1990 Super Bowl. *"I think my attitude is the reason I'm so successful on the football field. I simply concentrate on the defensive backs all week, study their every move — how each player is going to react when a receiver with a ball comes his way."*

16

Then he choreographs his own moves at least three days before the game. *"I visualize everything that's going to happen in the football game. I know exactly what I am going to do, how I'm going to run the pattern on each defensive back. I've got it down to the last step."*

Ageless George Foreman visualized on the canvas of his mind exactly what he would do to regain the world heavyweight boxing championship long before he met Michael Moore in the ring. He rehearsed every move, every punch, every detail, over and over again in his mind. Foreman prepared his nerves and motor memory to act for him during the stress of the actual fight. *And when the moment came, his mind and body reacted magnificently. Foreman was hailed the new heavyweight boxing champion of the world.*

Research indicates mental practice is as effective as real practice. In fact, some psychologists say, in some situations, it's better. Psychologists designed an experiment to increase the success of basketball players in making free throws. Three groups were identified.

Group One practiced actually shooting free throws as instructed by coaches for 30 minutes every day for two weeks.

Group Two only imagined themselves shooting free throws as instructed by coaches for 30 minutes every day for two weeks. They imagined every detail. They saw the goal in their mind's eye. They felt the leather of the ball between their hands. They smelled the odors of the gym. They felt the contraction of muscles as their body propelled the ball toward the goal. They saw the perfect arch of the ball and heard the swish as it dropped cleanly through the net. They smiled at their perfect shot — all in their imagination.

Group Three did not practice at all — either physically or mentally.

At the end of two weeks, all three groups were tested for increased percentage of success at the free throw line. The results showed that Group Two, which had practiced only in their imaginations, had improved their percentages as much as Group One, which had actually practiced shooting free throws. Group Three showed no improvement.

Interesting — but what does it mean? One thing it means is that all salespeople can use their imagination to increase their success! You can become more articulate by imagining yourself being articulate in specific situations. You can become more forceful by imagining yourself acting in more forceful ways.

You can become more persuasive by imagining yourself acting in more persuasive ways. Mental practice creates a response that integrates those actions into your behavior. They become automatic.

You become excellent in selling when your selling techniques are mastered and become automatic. *The surest and quickest way to this proficiency is frequent mental rehearsal.* A few minutes of mental practice, seized any time — seized now — will make a big difference.

Golfing great, Paul Azinger, said, *"People are right when they say that golf is a mental game. Golf courses are significantly different. The quality of play is not markedly different. The key is how I feel about myself. When I think better, I play better."* Azinger should know. He had to prove his grit in overcoming the odds, struggling with cancer, to return to championship play.

Mary Crowley, a highly successful saleswoman and founder of Home Interiors, a nationwide company, frequently said, *"It's a fact that excellence in selling begins with having a strong image of what you intend to do. You can achieve what your mind can conceive."* If you see it in your imagination, you will do it.

Get a clear, distinctive picture of what you intend to do. Mentally rehearse it until it becomes automatic. You'll have begun your path to excellence in selling.

Directed visualization precedes and causes selling success. You are under the influence of what you have imagined every minute of your selling day. Your results correspond to the mental picture you carry in your mind.

Turn your "imagination dial" to the most desired scene. Spell out a detailed, vivid action shot of yourself as the salesperson you have always wanted to be. Rehearse that scene over and over in your mind. Let it become the real you!

> *I will bring you success or failure.*
> *I can work for or against you.*
> *I can make you a winner or a loser.*
> *I control the way you feel and the way you act.*
> *I cause you to be positive, optimistic and enthused.*
> *Or, I will make you discouraged, depressed and defeated.*
> *I can be nurtured, changed and replaced.*
> *I can never be removed.*
> *I am your imagination.*
> *Why not get to know me better?*

Positioning Precept
Visualize Desired Outcomes

Expect The Best

*The most rewarding things you do in life are
often the ones that look like they cannot be done.*

-Arnold Palmer

You've heard it said, "What you see is what you get." Consider this alternative: *What you expect is what you get.* Therefore, expect great things of yourself. Expect the best!

Don't cheat yourself out of high achievement. Expect it!

The bumble bee doesn't know it is aerodynamically impossible for him to fly. He simply expects it of himself!

The ant doesn't know he can't. And there goes another rubber tree plant! He simply expects it of himself.

What about you? What do you expect of yourself? Are you in the army of the ant or the swarm of the bumblebee who doesn't know he can't? Or do you limit yourself by staying within restrictive boundaries?

Dr. Denis Waitley challenges you, *"Make your goals out of reach ... but never out of sight."* Meggido Message has said, *"If you have accomplished all you planned for yourself, you have not planned enough."* Don't limit yourself by planning only that which is possible to accomplish. Expect more! Expect great things of yourself. Expect the best!

Arnold Palmer's statement that the most rewarding things you do in life are often the ones that look like they can't be done points you in the right direction. Expect to do those things that look like they can't be done. That's the source of highest satisfaction.

That's exhilaration!

A stream cannot rise higher than its fountainhead. Your fountainhead is your expectation of yourself. Set those expectations high. They will be the limit to which you rise.

And when those expectations are set high, begin to do the little things required to reach those goals. *Doing little things well is a necessary step toward doing big things with excellence.*

Romana Banuelos had little reason to expect great things for her life. When she was just 16 years old, living in Mexico, her husband deserted her and her two children. She was poverty-stricken and uneducated. But the day she found herself alone and penniless, she began to expect great things of herself.

Romana borrowed enough money to buy bus tickets for herself and her two children to Los Angeles, California. She spoke no English. She had no skills or training.

She arrived in Los Angeles with only seven dollars in her pocket. When she gave the address of a distant relative to a cab driver, it took her last dime to pay the cab fare.

Safe with her relatives, Romana began her search for a life of meaning. *Though beaten down, disappointed, and rejected, she held on to her great expectations for a better life.*

She got a job washing dishes in a cafe. After the evening shift was over, she stayed on from midnight to six o'clock in the morning to make tacos. Romana was able to save $400 which she invested in a taco machine. She expected great things of herself! During the next 20 years she developed the largest wholesale Mexican food business in the world, Romana's Mexican Food Products.

But that is not the end of the great expectations of Romana Banuelos. Because of her outstanding accomplishments, she was frequently cited by the business community. Ultimately, the President of the United States appointed her Secretary of the Treasury - the first Mexican-American and the sixth woman to hold the position.

Romana Banuelos had a dream. She expected great things of herself. She expected the little things she did to be done very well. And those little things done well paved the way for big things done with excellence.

What about you? Do you expect great things of yourself? Do you expect to do the little things very well? Do you expect those little things done well to pave the way to big things done with excellence? *Expect great things of yourself!*

Positioning Precept
Expect The Best

Keep A Positive Attitude

*My greatest discovery. We become what
we think about most of the time.*

-Earl Nightingale

Of the many words in all the languages of the world, what word would you say is the most important when it comes to this business of selling successfully?

Well, according to the experts, the word is "attitude." *It's a fact that this word — or rather, what we mean by this word — will determine, more than any other single thing, what happens to us.* The dictionary defines the word "attitude" as a noun meaning "position, disposition, or manner with regard to a person or thing."

And it is our attitude that determines what happens to us in selling. As William James of Harvard once put it, *"It's our attitude at the beginning of a task which, more than anything else will affect its successful outcome."* What he meant was that the kind of attitude we have when we make the initial contact with a prospect will determine to a large extent whether or not we'll be successful on that call.

Each of us has a choice, no matter what the circumstances may be — to be either positive or not. There is absolutely nothing to be gained by not being enthusiastic, so why even consider it. If you keep the right attitude, it's amazing how quickly the "audience" changes — how sales start to go your way — and how lucky you seem to become.

No study or discussion of attitude and its impact on your success in selling can be considered complete without examining the ways the mind can mislead you.

Our minds are not always truth-finding instruments. Sometimes our minds serve to protect us from hearing the truth when it can discourage or damage us. This can happen in these four ways:

1) **The mind forgets what is negative and has the tendency to remember the positive.** We tend to remember what we want to remember. Most of the time, these are the positive issues.

   When gathering data during experiments, Albert Einstein made it a point to write down anything that contradicted a theory. This would protect him from his own mind subconsciously tucking it away in the file of "forgotten things." He had no trouble remembering the things supportive of the theory he was trying to prove.

2) **The mind is suggestible.** You tend to find what you expect. The Department of Health in Evanston, Illinois, one time announced an installation of a new chlorination system to purify the city's water. The water purification system was to be in operation by June 10th. On June 11th, the city began to receive complaint after complaint that the "water was not fit to drink." The "new product" was not acceptable; the press even picked up on it. For over a week, the Board of Health made no mention that a problem had delayed the installation of the new system. *When the purification system became operational later, there were no complaints!*

3) **The mind rationalizes.** You can find reasons to justify what you want to do or say. The mind will assist you in justifying your position.

4) **The mind rebels at new ideas and new methods.** Our tendency is to cling to the status quo, or to existing conditions. To avoid change is a common human trait. It's a trait which comes with our birth certificate. We all grow comfortable with existing conditions, even those we dislike.

To make sound choices, to be well-adjusted and achieve success in selling, react to things as they are, not as you wish they were, or even as your mind will let you believe they are.

Positive results make selling more enjoyable, and positive thinking leads to positive results. *We become what we think about most of the time.*

Somewhere we came across General Colin Powell's philosophies for helping him keep his thinking correct. We thought these were good.

- *It can be done! Make this your motto.*
- *Use perpetual optimism as a force multiplier.*
- *Be careful what you choose. You may get it.*
- *Don't let adverse facts stand in the way of a good decision.*
- *Check out the small things.*
- *Don't take counsel of your fears. Remain calm.*
- *Share credit.*
- *Avoid having your ego so close to your position that when your position falls, your ego goes with it.*
- *Sometimes being responsible means people will be mad at you.*
- *It ain't as bad as you think. It will look better in the morning.*

Positioning Precept
Keep A Positive Attitude

Build A Strong Self-Image

As is our confidence, so is our capacity.

-William Hazily

The late Dr. Maxwell Maltz, the father of *Psycho-Cybernetics*, taught the students at our Purdue Management School all about self-image psychology. *"You will always be true to your self-concept,"* the plastic surgeon would point out, *"But, your self-concept can and does change."* — I can't sell this stuff. Selling is easy

Whether you realize it or not, you constantly carry a mental image of yourself as a salesperson. This "image of self" may be vague, ill-defined and even blurred in your conscious thinking. You may be at a loss to clearly explain and define this mind's-eye picture. You may even deny its existence. *But it is there, complete in every detail, in your subconscious mind. This self-image or mind's-eye picture is your private and personal conception of "what kind of a person I am."*

Your self-image is made up out of two perceptions you hold in your mind about yourself. These two perceptions are (1) "What I've Got" (WIG), and (2) "What It Takes" (WIT). These perceptions have, for the most part, been formed from your total experiences up to this point in life. Every emotion, thought, observation, feeling, word spoken or heard, expression, joy, triumph, sorrow, humiliation, success or failure plays a part in shaping these two perceptions.

WIG I know people will be Trusting
WIT I will have to push most people to make a claim.

Once any idea or belief is accepted as a part of this picture, it becomes a "basic truth" to you - regardless of its validity - and influences your overall judgment in that area. All of your actions, reactions, thoughts, beliefs, opinions and abilities are consistent with this mind's-eye picture. It shapes and colors everything you think, do, say and are. *You unavoidably "act like" the person you "see" yourself to be.* In fact, it is practically impossible for you to act in any other manner. Your mind's-eye picture influences your willpower, which in turn controls all your conscious effort.

These all-important WIG and WIT mind's-eye pictures exercise primary control over the "goal-seeking mechanisms" of your subconscious mind. They rule your behavior and, of course, are based upon vast amounts of data "programmed" into the memory storage area of your subconscious mind.

Every individual carries around a definite mental picture of "What I've Got" and "What It Takes." *These two perceptions determine your self-concept.* And since you perform consistently in accordance with this self-concept, you must form the habit of consciously controlling the WIG and WIT pictures on your "mind's screen."

You exercise control over these pictures by reading books, listening to cassettes, viewing videos and associating with positive thinking, optimistic individuals. You are what you watch, listen to and read. *Form the habit of devoting your time and energy to positive people, thoughts and experiences.* Surround yourself with Positive, or you will subject to the negative

Psychologists believe that by the time you reach the age of two, 50 percent of what you believe about yourself has been formed. By the time you're six, 60% of your belief about yourself is established. By the time you reach the age of 14, 99% of your self-image is firmly in place. Your early experiences seem to have hammered that image into a distinct shape and form. Growing up, shy, not very talkative

Yet, it's not your experiences that have created your self-image. I've had It's what you believe about yourself as a result of those experiences that form your self-image. to break down those walls + reform my self image

Check your beliefs about yourself. Ask yourself these questions:

[handwritten: 9-step]   *[handwritten: I have to have a ton of information to feel comfortable]*

- Do I see myself as competent and well-informed? *[handwritten: to feel comfortable]*
- Do I see myself as one who is capable of making significant contributions? *[handwritten: — Are you helping — express my opinion]*
- Do I feel good about who I am and what I'm doing? *[handwritten: — Do you like the product & what it provides]*

Our beliefs about what is possible — or impossible — often become a self-fulfilling prophecy. Until Dr. Roger Bannister ran a mile in less than four minutes, everyone concluded it was impossible. Soon after, the four-minute mile became almost routine. Did the competing runners become more physically fit? The experts say no. Once the athletes believed it was possible, it was possible. In fact, it was expected. We can point to similar examples throughout the world of selling.

Count as an enemy the person who shakes your expectation of your selling ability. Remember, as a professional salesperson your self-confidence is the one thing you can never afford to surrender. Nothing multiplies a salesperson's ability like faith in himself or herself. It will make a one-talent person into a success — while a ten-talent person without it will fail. *[handwritten: Tyler - gift of gab full confidence — Travis - Talent no confidence]*

How often have you heard this said about some successful person, "Everything he or she touches turns to gold?" We sometimes think of successful people as being lucky. The fact is, their success represents their expectations - it's the sum of their habitual ways of thinking. By the force of their expectations, such persons wring success from the most adverse circumstances.

Expectation brings successful experiences and successful experiences reinforce the power of confidence in selling. *[handwritten: — We all know that]*

Individuals who are self-reliant, positive, optimistic and assured "magnetize" conditions. They carry in their very presence an air of victory that compounds its power by convincing others. Their poise, assurance and abilities increase in direct ratio to the number of selling achievements. *[handwritten: Remind of Ty — raving self-love]*

Here is a five-step process for building a strong self-image:

1) **Learn to forgive yourself.** It's important not to carry
   around a guilt complex. Forgive yourself for the little
   human errors you have made in the past.

   Don't dwell on your imperfections. Recognize your good
   points and be proud of them.

   Pamper yourself a little more. You can't be a likable
   person unless you like yourself. It's almost impossible to
   like yourself if you cannot discover the way to forgive
   yourself. *Don't Sweat the small stuff.*

2) **Be able to forgive others.** Don't carry grudges. Remember, you become what you think about. If you carry a *focus on*
   grudge, you're likely to become like the person you are *the positive*
   carrying the grudge against. *Don't be a bastard*
   Try to be Happy go Lucky

3) **Develop your ability to communicate.** Express how you
   feel. We have all experienced the situation where we carry
   something around inside and all of a sudden decide to
   express it. We jump all over someone — maybe someone
   very close to us. However, when it comes out, we feel
   better and they feel better. It is important to communicate
   with others, especially those close to you: your spouse,
   children and friends. Don't carry feelings inside. Let them
   come out. *[This is important makes thanker feel good as well + it*
   Don't be modest in the way you accept compliments. If *Opens up*
   someone gives you a compliment, thank the person. Com- *even bigger*
   municate how good he or she made you feel. *doors of*
   solid comune

   It is also important to communicate with yourself. In this
   regard, ask yourself these questions: "When was the last
   time I was alone? When was the last time I just sat around
   and thought about my situation?"

4) **Build a life model.** Push the calendar ahead five years. Ask yourself where you expect to be professionally in those 60 short months. It's important to put in writing the type of person you want to become as well as the things you want to accomplish. Then decide what must be done this year and this quarter.

5) **Compete, but don't compare.** You should compete with your friends and associates, but you never compare. "Keeping up with the Joneses" adds unneeded pressures to your selling life. *Build your life model; compare your life with what you ought to be.* Many people are frustrated and become discouraged because they are comparing themselves with other people. Never compare yourself with others — compete with them.

Self-image is the source of confidence. In selling, your confidence is the measure of your capacity.

Positioning Precept
Build A Strong Self-Image

Nobody will Love you
Until you Love yourself
Therefore nobody will fee
comfortable buying from
you if they don't
Trust or Like you
or the feel uneasy

Practice Optimism

*There is very little difference in people,
but that little difference makes a big difference.*

-W. Clement Stone

Optimism is the constant companion of high-performing sales-people. It's their trademark, their way of life. *Optimism is the difference that makes a big difference.*

The traditional formula for success has looked something like this:

Talent + Motivation = Success

Psychologist Martin Seligman suggests some new formulas:

Talent + Motivation + Optimism = Success

Talent + Motivation + Pessimism = Failure

The idea is that you can have both talent and motivation and still fail if you don't have optimism. The critical ingredient in the success formula is optimism.

Talent has been shown to be largely inherent. It's not something you learn. You can sharpen it. You can focus it, but it is depressingly hard to increase.

Motivation can be boosted rather easily. In a 30-second bite, clever advertising can motivate you to buy. Motivational speakers and seminars pump up participants to exuberance. The trouble is more pumping is needed in a week or a month.

Metropolitan Life discovered a measure of optimism was a more effective predictor of a sales rep's survival and success than career assessment profiles. *Sales reps with the highest optimism scores produced the highest dollar volume.* Those were the agents who made the second and third call, and the fourth and fifth call. And they made each optimistically.

The constant — the critical factor — in the success formula is optimism! *And we have good news for you. It can be learned.* Yes, learned! It can be learned in such a way that it doesn't fade or dissipate. It can become a way of life. It can become a valuable partner.

Optimism is a way of thinking. It's not a feeling. Motivation tends to be based on how you feel about something. Optimism is based on how you think about a situation. You can learn to think optimistically.

The thought patterns of optimists go something like this:

- *I got the sale! And there will be some additional business, too.*

    or

- I didn't get the appointment, but that was only one call. The next call should be a better one.

- *I had a great start. It's going to be a great week!*

    or

- I've had a slow start. The balance of the week is sure to be much better.

- *I was really effective in closing that sale.*

    or

- I missed on that one. They wouldn't have bought from anyone today.

Optimists believe good events are going to continue. Bad events are transitory. "*I have not failed 10,000 times. I have successfully found 10,000 ways that will not work.*" That's an optimist's response. The optimist's name: Thomas A. Edison.

Optimists believe good events will pervade everything they do. Bad events are singular and isolated.

Optimists accept that they are responsible for the good things that happen in their careers. They feel bad events are the result of circumstances beyond their influence.

You can learn to think optimistically. The result is energy. The result is eagerness to make the next call. The result is enthusiasm on that interview. The result is success!

Positioning Precept
Practice Optimism

Make Every Occasion A Great Occasion

*I'm given credit for some genius. All the genius
I have lies in this; when I have a subject in hand, I
study it profoundly. Day and night it is before me.
My mind becomes pervaded with it. Then the effort
which I have made is what people are pleased to call
the fruit of genius. It is the fruit of labor and thought.*

-Alexander Hamilton

The plaque on the wall reads: "*Make every occasion a great
occasion. You never know when someone is taking your measure
for a higher position — including, of course, buying your product
or service.*" Every occasion — even an unwanted, time-consuming interruption — can be transformed into a great occasion.
How? *Simply by viewing the event through the lens of an expect-
ant, determined, creative attitude.*

The prospect calls and cancels an appointment at the last minute.
A great occasion? Hardly. But wait! Turn that temporary setback
into a profitable event. Use those few free minutes to take stock of
the situation. Remind yourself, the prospect is now obligated a bit
more. Also, use this freed-up time to make those contact or public
relation calls you've wanted to make. These positive moves will
make a difference.

Interruptions, for example, can be perceived as sources of irritation
or opportunities for service; as moments lost or experiences
gained. They can annoy or enrich you; get under your skin or give
you a shot in the arm, depending on your attitude toward them.

Emerson wrote, *"This time, like all times, is a very good time if we but know what to do with it."* No occasion is a "little" occasion.

No moment is insignificant. No person is unimportant. This call, this interview, this presentation, this situation can become a great occasion if you choose to make it so!

Here's The Professional Sales Rep's Creed we came across one time. It's a good one to adopt.

The Professional Sales Rep's Creed

To respect my profession, my company and myself. To be honest in all of my dealings with my company, as I expect my company to be honest and fair with me; to think of it with loyalty, speak of it with praise, and act always as a trustworthy custodian of its good name. To be an individual whose word is believed and respected.

To base my expectations of reward on a solid foundation of contributions made; to be willing to pay the price of success in honest, intelligent effort. To look upon my job as an opportunity to display enthusiasm and optimism.

To remember sales success lies within myself, in my own mind, my own energy. To expect difficulties and work my way through them; to turn hard experience into capital for future struggles.

To believe in what I'm selling. To sell ethically; to kill doubts with strong convictions and reduce any friction with an agreeable personality.

To make a study of my business or line; to know my profession in every detail from the ground up; to mix brains with my efforts and use systems and methods in my work. To find time to do everything needed by never letting time find me doing nothing.

To keep my future unmortgaged by debt; to save money as well as earn it; to eliminate spending habits; to steer clear of dissipation and guard my high energy level as my competitive edge.

To take a good grip on the joy of life; to fight against nothing so hard as my own weaknesses, and to endeavor to grow professionally and personally with the passage of every selling day.

Finally, to be fully committed to achieve excellence in sales.

In a time when we've grown to almost deify leisure time, it's good for me to remember my greatest satisfactions will revolve around the level of excellence I achieve in my sales job. This I believe.

This is my creed.

Positioning Precept
Make Every Occasion A Great Occasion

Fail Forward

You've got to put failure to work for you.

-Thomas J. Watson, Jr.

The subject was strikeouts and walks. During his career with the Yankees, the late, great Mickey Mantle had 1,710 strikeouts and 1,734 walks. *"That's 3,444 times I came to bat without hitting the ball,"* Mickey said. *"Figure 500 at-bats a season for a player playing regularly — and that means I played seven years without hitting the ball."* That's a lot of swings, attempts and difficulties to overcome for one of the most respected batting champions baseball has ever known.

Mantle continued, *"Sometimes when I'm doing a question-and-answer, a guy will ask, 'Didn't you strikeout a lot?' I say, 'I sure did. I struck out 1,710 times, but every one of them was almost a home run.'"* This is the type of attitude which carries athletes and salespeople to greatness.

Difficulties bring out your best qualities and make greatness possible. The superior selling performances you admire usually take place because the individual subscribes to a selling philosophy we call the "Fail Forward — It's Always Too Early to Give Up" philosophy. When you "Fail Forward" you learn from your experience. You strengthen your resolve. And, you move steadfastly toward your goals.

Studies reveal that 58 percent — more than half — of all sales people quit completely after a single call on a prospect. Another 20 percent make two calls before giving up and seven percent make three calls. The remaining 22 percent make five calls or more, and these are the stars we honor because they produce about 75 percent of all the business. *To achieve success, you must first endure difficulty.* If you somehow find yourself successful without having been severely tested, it's only because someone suffered through the obstacles before you. This is true in every walk of life, but we believe it's especially true in selling.

It's not what happens to you as a salesperson — but what you do after it happens — that makes the big difference in your selling life. That's why selling success depends far more on mental attitude than it does on mental capacity. *It's the salesperson who uses difficulty, not the one who avoids it, who grows and goes to the top in the company.* No salesperson is immune to trouble. Everyone faces obstacles and disappointments. They are a part of business life, a part of the process of living and growing! These negative happenings can make or break you, depending on how you take them and use them to "Fail Forward."

Imagine the Hall Of Fame Golf Professional, Betsy King, insisting that all the hazards be removed from the course before she plays. Level all the bunkers, fill all the sand traps, straighten out the doglegs, fill all the water holes and have no out-of-bounds. What pro do you know who would want to play on that kind of course? *The easy course is not the interesting one and, naturally, the pro knows it will never develop his or her best game because it has no challenge — no difficulties which must be faced and overcome.*

A feature story on Fred Astaire included a quote from a critic's review early in his "sales" career. "Can't act. Can't sing. Balding. Can dance a little." Such is the story of life. Such is the story of selling. The important question is whether or not you allow difficulties to bring out the best in you. Do you "Fail Forward?" Fred Astaire certainly did!

Opposing circumstances create selling strength. Fear of opposition will help to keep you up tight, rob you of drive and take the edge off your selling effectiveness. Customer opposition and competition will make you stronger. *That's why your reward for success in selling will not be what you gain from it, but rather what you become because of it.* The salesperson who triumphs over difficulties bears the sign of victory on his or her face. An "air of victory" is apparent with his or her every selling action.

Marguerite Piazza, the well-known Metropolitan Opera star, had "mountains of difficulties" to make her a person of great strength. Happily married, a promising career, and the mother of six healthy children — a perfect picture, yet it was shattered at the snap of a finger. Her husband died suddenly, and at almost the same time, a spot on her cheek was diagnosed as melanoma, a deadly cancer.

It's not what happens to you, but what you do after it happens that makes the difference in your success. Marguerite Piazza, responsible for six children and facing life alone, had her cheek removed and endured damaging radiation. But she sang! And she sang, and she sang — unwilling to stop doing what she loved most to do. She overcame her difficulties. Greatness was hers.

The everlasting battle to win success in spite of every barrier is the price Marguerite paid — and it's what you must pay to enjoy extraordinary selling achievements. That's why the statement on the gridiron at West Point will be meaningful to you: "On these friendly fields of strife are sown the seeds that on other fields and in other days will be born the fruits of victory."

Positioning Precept
Fail Forward

Never Give Up

*When you reach the end of your rope,
tie a knot and hang on!*

-Cyrus Hall

A solid base for success is perseverance. Dismissed from a major newspaper with the advice to try something else because he had no talent, a young man considered giving up. But he didn't. His name ... Walt Disney. Another young man who loved flying, crash landed the first two times he soloed and, the third time, he flew head-on into another aircraft. Give up? Not Admiral Richard Byrd. Author Rod Serling of *Twilight Zone* fame, wrote and tried to market 40 stories before he sold one. *Yes, a solid base for success is perseverance.*

The great triumphs of your sales career will be the rewards of your persistence. Never depend on your genius to carry you. If you have talent, improve it. If you have none, develop it. But do not depend on it. *The rewards of selling are the results of persistence.*

The Golden Arches are a universal sign recognized throughout the world. Ronald McDonald is a household name. The result of talent? Perhaps. But more than that, it is the result of the motto adopted by McDonald executives: *"Press on!"*

Perseverance, not genius, separates winners from the losers in selling. Sixty percent or more of your selling time is spent in a negative environment. Three of every five prospects you call on will likely deflate your ego. It's perseverance that serves you in such a climate. Never give up!

The shortest and most powerful commencement address ever given included those three words. Sir Winston Churchill approached the podium at Oxford University with his usual props — a cigar, a cane, and a top hat. The crowd rose in thunderous applause. With unmatched dignity, he settled the audience and stood confident before his admirers. He ritually removed his hat and placed it on the podium. He hung his cane nearby. He removed the stub of a cigar from his mouth and laid it down.

Churchill gazed a moment at the crowd. They were poised and eager to hear his message. Then, with authoritative voice, he shouted, *"Never, never, never, never, never give up!"* The thunderstruck crowd stared. Then Churchill rose on his toes and shouted a second time, *"Never, never, never, never, never give up!"* The audience sat in stunned silence. Mr. Churchill reached for his hat and his cigar, steadied himself with his cane, and left the platform. His message had been clearly communicated in those seven words. His speech was finished and what a memorable speech it was.

Filmmaker Bud Greenspan tells the story of packing up his cameras after the men's marathon at Mexico City Olympics. Suddenly, a reporter ran up to him. *"You ought to film this one,"* the man said, as Greenspan looked up.

Into the darkened stadium hobbled a participant, his right leg bandaged in two places. If you saw the "re-play" on television, you'll remember he winced with every step. *The race had been over for more than an hour, but John Stephen Akhwari of Tanzania still ran.* The few hundred spectators who had lingered in the stadium began to clap, slowly and steadily, as Akhwari struggled to the finish line. When finally he stumbled across the finish line, clutching his damaged leg with both hands, the small crowd roared.

Greenspan had recorded every painful, triumphant moment of that emotional, courageous finish. *"I asked him, 'Why'd you do this? You were in such pain, and you couldn't win,'"* Greenspan recalled. *"He looked at me like I was crazy. 'Mr. Greenspan, I don't think you understand. My country did not send me 5,000 miles to start the race. They sent me 5,000 miles to finish it!'"*

Herman Sherman developed this Code of Persistence for sales-people. It's good!

I resolve to:

- *Never give up so long as I know I am right.*
- *Believe all things will work out if I hang on until the end.*
- *Remain courageous and confident when the odds turn against me.*
- *Never permit anyone to intimidate me or shake my belief in me.*
- *Fight to overcome any physical handicaps and set backs.*
- *Try again and again and yet again to reach my dreams.*
- *Take new faith and resolve from the knowledge that many successful men and women have had to fight defeat and adversity to achieve their greatness.*

In the Far East, people plant a tree they call The Chinese Bamboo. During the first four years, they water and fertilize the plant with seemingly little or no results. The fifth year they continue to apply water and fertilizer — and in five weeks' time the tree grows 90 feet in height! The obvious question is did the bamboo tree grow 90 feet in five weeks or did it grow 90 feet in five years? The answer is apparent. It grew 90 feet in five years. *During those five years, if at any time the people had quit watering and fertilizing the tree, it would have died.*

Success in selling depends on your willingness to do exactly that. Never give up! Selling is a delayed-profit business. When you run the power mower over the lawn, the grass is cut — immediately. You see it. When you strike the right keys on the organ, pleasing sounds are heard — immediately. You hear it. But in selling, there is not always immediate results. *The reward is frequently delayed. Persistence is demanded. Nothing takes the place of persistence. Nothing is rewarded more in selling than persistence.*

Positioning Precept
Never Give Up!

Precept Supporting Philosophies

To be successful, you have to have your heart in your business and your business in your heart.
—Thomas Watson, Sr.

There is nothing either good or bad, but thinking makes it so.
— Shakespeare

Some people like people who win. Some people hate people who win. But people who win will never go unnoticed.
— Mike Krzyzewski, Duke University Basketball Coach

No one can make you feel inferior without your consent.
— Eleanor Roosevelt

Things are seldom what they seem. Skim milk masquerades as cream.   — Warren E. Buffett

Our self-image prescribes the limits for the accomplishment of any particular goals. It prescribes the 'area of the possible.'
— Dr. Maxwell Maltz

The only thing that stands between an individual and what he or she wants from life is often the will to try it and the faith to believe it is possible.   — Richard M. DeVos

Good enough never is; and better is only acceptable if there is commitment to make it better.
— Betsy Sanders

Things turn out best for the individuals who are determined to make the best of the way things turn out.
— John Wooden

Off The Professionals' Bookshelf

Allen, James. *As A Man Thinketh.* Fleming Revell Company, 1957.

Bettger, Frank. *How I Raised Myself from Failure to Success in Selling.* Prentice-Hall, 1949.

Briner, Bob. *Squeeze Play.* Zondervan, 1993.

Conwell, Russell. *Acres Of Diamonds.* Harper, 1960.

Goldratt, Eliyahu. *The Goal.* North River Press, 1995.

Helmstetter, Shad. *What To Say When You Talk To Yourself.* Pocket Books, 1986.

Leider, Richard. *The Power Of Purpose.* Fawcett Books.

Maltz, Dr. Maxwell. *Psycho-Cybernetics.* Prentice-Hall, 1988

Schwartz, David. *The Magic Of Thinking Big.* Simon & Schuster, 1986.

Selismary, Ph.D., Martin E.P. *Learned Optimism.* Alfred A. Knopf, 1991

Stone, W. Clement. *Success Through A Positive Mental Attitude.* Prentice-Hall, 1960.

Waitley, Denis. *Empires Of The Mind.* W. Morris, 1995.

Ziglar, Zig. *Over The Top.* Oliver Nelson, 1994.

Section Two
Work Habit Strengtheners

Do your work. Not just your work and no more, but a little more
for the lavishing sake. That little more which is worth all the rest.
And when you suffer as you must, and if you sometimes doubt as
you will — do your work. Put your heart into it. Give it your best.
The sky will one day clear.

Then out of your very doubt and suffering will be born
the supreme joy that comes from work well done.

In a day and time when we have grown to almost deify leisure
time, it's good to be reminded that many of our greatest satisfac-
tions in life will come, not from our leisure, but from our work.

-Dean Briggs

Think Success

*It's through their work that most individuals write the
story of their lives. They are both the author and the
story's principal character. They are free to be the
hero or the villain; to be a success or failure.*

-Malcolm Forbes

Your mind is an amazing piece of equipment. When your mind
works one way, it carries you to certain success in selling. But the
same mind operating in a different way will produce a total failure.

Right from the start, condition your mind to consider this question
often, *"Is this the way a successful salesperson does it?"* You can
use this mental prompter to keep you thinking right and to make
you a successful performer, a leader in your field.

Ask specifically, is this the way a successful salesperson would:

- dress?
- plan the sales day?
- build relationships?
- develop contacts?
- handle the telephone?
- study and prepare?
- practice his or her sales talk?
- present a proposal?
- close the sale?
- ask for endorsements?
- keep records?

*In as many selling situations as you can, ask yourself these kinds of
questions.* Upgrading your thinking upgrades your actions and this
leads to success.

Remember, how you think determines how you act. How you act determines how your prospects and customers react to you.

Burn this dominant theme into your mind. It's this: *enthusiasm is infectious. It attracts customers.*

It's always great to watch a salesperson who is alive. Put the high achieving sales rep's success story under the microscope. You'll always find that sustained enthusiasm is a big chunk of it. A spirited optimism is a keynote of the truly effective salesperson.

Any decision of how to achieve success in selling would be incomplete without reference being made to the importance habits play in our everyday performance.

We are all creatures of habit — and that's not bad. Without habits, we could hardly function normally, let alone accomplish much.

But unfortunately, there's always the tendency to develop bad habits and especially so in a job where there is no place to "punch in or punch out" and where you are not likely to be closely regimented.

A habit is a learned pattern of acting — a way of behaving that has become routine.

Mathematicians comparing the human brain to the computer have calculated that in an average lifetime of 70 years, the human being can take in and remember about 100 billion bits. A bit is a measure of information — the smallest piece of data capable of being stored in a computer.

That enormous number represents far more information than even the most advanced computer can handle. A computer, when it receives as much information as it can deal with, simply quits receiving information. It can't take in and process any more. The human brain reacts similarly. When it has received as much information as it can cope with, it "turns off." It stops paying attention.

But this marvelous mechanism has the ability to receive and store, in long-term memory, information about how to perform routine tasks, and to recall and use that information without having to think consciously about it. These routine actions are habits. Consider this. You normally don't have to think about tying your shoes, riding a bicycle, walking or remembering your address or telephone number.

Apparently, from what researchers can determine, we record each experience we have — each response we make to various stimuli. The more times we respond to certain stimuli in the same way, the more "worn" the neural circuits and pathways in the brain and nervous system become.

At last, the memory is able to trigger an automatic response, thought or feeling to a specific stimulus. Repetition is the key.

It follows then, that doing something the right way enough times — properly planning tomorrow's priorities each day, properly executing a telephone track, a sales presentation, or a step-by-step closing strategy — builds good habits. Conversely, if you choose the wrong option enough times, you'll form bad habits.

The earlier the conditioning, the stronger the influence. In other words, it's easier for you to build good habits early in your selling career than to break bad ones later on.

The way in is easy — the way out is hard!

Positioning Precept
Think Success

Plan Productive Days

*High-potential selling activities must always be
concretely planned the day before. This is how you
make certain you wake up employed. Make this a
habit and you'll find there will be few "unassigned
moments" during your peak selling time.*

-Robert Shook

Have you ever heard of the simple planning idea for which a man
was paid $25,000? It was an idea that helped build one of the
country's largest industries. It has since been used profitably by
hundreds of top flight salespeople. It will work wonders for
anyone who puts it to use.

Before we give you the $25,000 idea, let us remind you that a
successful life, or a successful sales year, is nothing more than a
collection of successful days.

A successful day consists of a series of successful acts. So, in
reducing a successful life to its most common denominator, you're
left with the individual acts you perform. A day is filled with all
sorts of acts. For our purposes, let's say the acts you perform can
be placed under two headings: 1) Productive acts, in that they
directly or indirectly contribute to your success in selling, and 2)
Non-productive acts.

*Naturally, to succeed you must increase the number of productive
acts, and at the same time, decrease the number of non-productive
acts.*

Baby sitting is a productive act for a teenager; mowing the lawn is
a productive act for the landscaper; running errands is profitable
for the delivery person. But none of these acts are productive for a

49

salesperson. *The only productive acts for you are those acts that pertain to your business. Those acts that put you in contact with a potential customer.* Therefore, it makes good sense to perform unproductive acts only during unproductive times: weekends, or after you're all through for the day. Try to use all of your prime time, your productive time, for the performance of productive acts only. This is often the difference between the success and the failure in this business.

If you spend the same amount of time on the job that is required of an individual working in a factory, you will be eminently success-ful, and your earnings will be far above average. But, being your own boss, you may tend to be far too lenient with yourself. Ask yourself if you devote a full eight-hour day to your sales job — eight full hours of acts devoted to your business — what kind of results will you constantly produce?

So, now — let us give you the $25,000 idea that will get you on the right track, and keep you there.

This story goes back to the time when Charles Schwab was Presi-dent of the Bethlehem Steel Company. He granted an interview to an efficiency expert named Ivy Lee. Lee was telling him how his firm could help him do a better job of managing the company when Mr. Schwab broke in to say that he wasn't managing as well as he knew how to. He said that what was needed wasn't more knowing — but a lot more doing. *"We know what to do. If you can show us a better way of getting it done, I'll listen — and pay you anything within reason you ask,"* Mr. Schwab said.

Lee then told Mr. Schwab to take a piece of paper, and he'd show him how to increase his productivity by 50 percent. Schwab looked as though he didn't believe him, but he did as requested.

Lee said, *"Now write on that paper the six most important things you should get done tomorrow."* This took a couple of minutes. *"Now number them in the order of their importance."* When this had been done, Lee said, *"Now put that piece of paper in your pocket. The first thing tomorrow morning, take it out and look at Number One. Don't look at the others, just Number One, and start working on it, and stay with it until it's completed. Then start on item Number Two. Don't let anything get you off the track; and handle it the same way. Then Number Three, and so on until you have to quit for the day. Don't worry if you've only finished one or two. You'll be working on the most important ones; the others can wait. If you can't finish them all by this method, you couldn't have finished them with any other. And without this system, you'd probably take ten times as long to do them, and might not even have them in the order of their importance."*

"Do this everyday," Lee went on. *"After you've convinced yourself of the value of this system, have your sales reps try it. Then send me your check for whatever you think the idea is worth."*

In a few weeks, Mr. Schwab sent Ivy Lee a check for $25,000 with a letter saying the lesson was the most profitable, from a money standpoint, that he had ever learned in his life. It helped make a then little known steel company into the biggest, independent producer in the world.

In sales, you're an independent producer, too. Try the $25,000 idea in your life. Try it for just 30 days, and don't wander from it. For the next month, begin every working day with a slip of paper containing the six most important acts you must perform that day. And start immediately on Number One; then go to Number Two; and so on. These are the most productive acts. And make certain they are taken care of first; that they get top billing. Only after they have been done can you afford the luxury of non-productive acts.

By following this simple, but enormously effective plan, you will guarantee the success of each day. And as each is completed, you will have placed one more vital building block firmly and effectively in place.

You'll be amazed at how quickly you'll reach your goal through this plan. It takes all the confusion and wasted time out of your days. You're always on target when you're working, and you're always working on the most important act.

Try it ... watch what happens in just 30 days. At the end of that time, we think you'll agree the idea is worth every penny of $25,000.

Positioning Precept
Plan Productive Days

Fix Action Plan

*No life ever grows great until it is
focused, dedicated and disciplined.*

-Harry Emmerson Fosdick

As we write these pages, Michael Jordan is at it again. The Chicago Bulls are chalking up a convincing win against the Dallas Mavericks. Jordan ends his night's work with 32 points. That's his NBA career scoring average — 32 points. It didn't matter what team he was facing, what injuries he was nursing, or who was guarding him, Jordan managed to get his 32 points.

Recently, a reporter asked Michael how he has maintained that consistency for nearly 11 seasons. Jordan's response is the most practical goal-achieving strategy we know anything about. Jordan said, *"Years ago, I simplified things. Thirty-two points per game is only eight points a quarter. I figure I will find some way each quarter to get eight points."*

This is a clear, simple approach for setting a high standard for yourself and then achieving it. Begin with the end in mind. Then break it down into easily achievable mini-goals, and focus on those numbers. *We call this goal attainment insurance — and it can make a big difference in your approach to goal setting in selling.*

Goal setting defines chief aims. Goal setting puts order in your selling life. It sets priorities. It makes focus possible. Done properly, goal setting always leads to commitment. And commitment makes everything you're up to worthwhile. *Goal setting is often a de-motivating practice unless it is broken down into doable components.* This is where you focus.

The two keys are commitment and focus. An individual with specific goals is an individual who will make a responsible commitment. *This is the person who believes a commitment made is a debt unpaid.* Effectiveness and productivity are greatly multiplied when one has singleness of purpose. Tunnel vision is good when targets are clearly identified.

Goal setting is the initial cause of which success is the final effect.

Now that you have an understanding of the importance of goal setting, what are some criteria for establishing your chief aims? Here are four characteristics critical to effective goal setting.

First, your goals must be achievable. Why push and strive toward a goal when you know it is outside of your reach? Properly established goals are attainable only with maximum effort. They have been set realistically high. They push you to your highest, but they must be attainable.

Second, your goals must be believable. This is closely related to the first criterion. They must reflect realism, not idealism. They must be something that you are convinced you can reach.

Third, your goals must be measurable. Think about your favorite athletic event. Would you find it to be interesting if they had no scoreboard? What makes football exciting is knowing the score and how much time is remaining. Your goals will become challenging only when they are measurable.

Fourth, your goals must have deadlines. Time is your most precious commodity. It can never be replaced. If you are to use your time most productively, your goals must have deadlines. Deadlines bring compulsion and a responsible commitment to a plan of action.

These are the four characteristics to sound goal setting — achievable, believable, measurable and deadlines. These are the four pillars that will support your chief aims.

Motivation occurs when dreams become goals and goals convert to responsible commitments. Commitments move you to tap the vast reservoirs of unused talent and potential you already possess.

High achievers fantasize, just as we encourage you to do. But they don't stop at dreaming — and neither should you. Crystallize your objectives. The future is where you dream. This year is where you live, sell and perform.

Yearly goals bridge the gap between where you presently are and where you intend to go in selling. They put you on schedule to achieve your career objectives. *Few people know what they want. Still fewer decide when they want it.*

As you establish your sales goals each year, you will find it very helpful to establish two kinds of goals —*committed minimum and superior.*

Your minimum goals are what you must do this year. They are what you will do regardless. *Your minimum goals are committed goals.* They are set realistically high and require a complete commitment to their achievement. *There is no room for compromise with your minimum goals. Here you make a responsible commitment.*

On the other hand, your superior goals are flavored with optimism. These are the numbers you hope to achieve. Those numbers you want to reach over and above your minimum goals. Superior goals are bonus goals.

Give careful thought to your minimum and superior goals. They are small keys that unlock big features in selling.

Sales Performance Plan For _____

Sales Rep _____ Date _____

KEY RESULT AREAS	COMMITMENT	SUPERIOR
Calls and Letters to New Prospects	_____	_____
Calls and Letters to Existing Customers	_____	_____
Total Contacts to New Prospects and Existing Customers	_____	_____
Call-To-Sale Ratio (total number of calls divided by total number of sales)	_____	_____
Presentations	_____	_____
Dollars Sold	$ _____	$ _____
Average Order Size	$ _____	$ _____
Referral Endorsements	_____	_____

SELF-DEVELOPMENT GOALS

The selling skills I will develop this year are the following:

_____

The knowledge I will acquire this year will be in these areas:

_____

The habits I will strengthen include the following:

_____

The most effective way for me to reach and surpass each of the above numbers is:

_____

A Commitment Made Is A Debt Unpaid

Next, you must fix a weekly plan of action that will insure your success. *A Weekly Effort Formula becomes indispensable.* Obviously, no pat formula can be developed which will be adaptable to everyone in business. The activity that is necessary for success varies according to your experience, background and contacts. This formula changes as you gain customers, experience, knowledge, skills and confidence.

It serves your best interest when your activity can be measured against a clearly defined standard. A Weekly Effort Formula, when calculated, can be an extremely helpful self-management tool for you. *Building the Weekly Effort Formula and adhering to it religiously is the equivalent of having "goal attainment insurance."*

Weekly Sales Effort Formula

Components	Must Do
Calls and Letters to New Prospects	_____
Calls and Letters to Existing Customers	_____
Total Number of Sales	_____
Presentations	_____
Dollars Sold	$ _____
Referral Endorsements	_____

Positioning Precept
Fix Action Plan

Develop Self-Discipline

What you do when you don't have to, determines exactly
what you'll be when you can no longer help it.

-Jack Murray

Several years ago in Philadelphia, Albert E. N. Gray delivered a speech to a group of sales people in which he defined The Common Denominator Of Success. Everyone expected him to say the usual things — that success comes as the result of hard work, commitment and the like. Instead, Gray introduced a success principle. He said, *"The common denominator of success, the secret for which so many salespeople have searched, lies in the fact that successful salespeople form the habit of doing the things failures don't like to do."* The successful are able to form the habit of doing the things that failures don't like to do because they are self-disciplined and motivated by satisfying results. The mediocre, the marginal and the unsuccessful are motivated by pleasing methods.

Disciplined salespeople are enthusiastic. They employ the magic of enthusiasm to inspire others to believe in them and to buy from them. They walk with a spring in their step. They sell with a sparkle in their eye. They speak with a note of confidence in their voice.

Disciplined salespeople are resourceful. They have imagination, initiative and fresh ideas. They are students who are always looking for the better way.

Disciplined salespeople are predictable and dependable. Their word is their bond and their acceptance of a challenge is always a forerunner of a job well-done. They can always be counted on, never counted out.

Disciplined salespeople are courageous. They stand for what they believe to be right, even in the midst of conflict and criticism. They dare to be an individual whose honor and integrity are respected and admired by all who know them.

Disciplined salespeople are persistent. They believe that "failure comes from following the line of least persistence."

Disciplined salespeople are optimistic. They have a reason for every success, not an excuse for every failure. Continually, they turn the impossible into the possible.

Disciplined salespeople are dedicated. They make a habit of being punctual and following through. Their motto is, "Let me help. How can I serve you?" They are conscientious but never contentious; determined but not dictatorial; dedicated but not demanding.

The difference between the stars in selling and the mediocre performers is about five minutes. Read that once again. The stars in selling spend five minutes more planning their activity and preparing their presentations. They invest five minutes more in research and study. They put five minutes more in prospecting and contacting prospective buyers. They are self-disciplined and this quality makes the difference.

Positioning Precept
Develop Self-Discipline

Be A Self-Starter

*Perhaps the most valuable result of all
education is the ability to make yourself do
the thing you have to do, when it ought to
be done, whether you like doing it or not.*

-Thomas Huxley

Nicholas Murray Butler, former Chancellor of Columbia University, once said, *"There are three kinds of people in the world today: Those who make things happen. Those who watch things happen. And those who have no idea of what is happening."* As a salesperson, you can distinguish yourself by having the ability to make things happen.

You were attracted to sales because you demonstrated a willingness to accept the responsibility for making desired results happen. Being accountable for making things happen and producing those desired results is invigorating. It gives real meaning to your sales job.

J. B. Conway, a great sales manager, once said, *"A good aim in your business life is not quite enough. Yesterday ended last night. Today you have to pull the trigger again."* The hardest job for most salespeople is pulling that trigger and getting started again. Getting started will no longer be difficult for you if you follow these simple steps: *First, resolve to have a victory every day. Second, have a well-conceived sales strategy. Work under the challenge of deadlines. Finally, visualize the rewards in your mind at all times.*

Salespeople who enjoy the reputation of knowing how to get a job done tell us the secret lies in forcing yourself to take that first step toward achieving some kind of victory today. Goethe put this truth into words which are sure to help you when you make them a part of your thinking. He said, *"Are you in earnest? Seize this very minute. What you can do, or dream you can, begin it! Boldness*

*has genius, power and magic in it. Only engage, and then the
mind grows heated. Begin, and the task is half completed."*

Don't wonder or ponder or contemplate too long. Don't wait until
you feel like it. Don't wait until you feel "hot." Don't wait until
conditions are just right. Instead, as Goethe suggests, *"begin it!"*

There's no better follow-up for a solid resolution than a clearly
spelled-out selling procedure. Mortimer Feinberg, the noted
psychologist, put it this way, *"You have to direct your efforts. You
have to channel your energies. Otherwise, all the energy and
output you generate is dissipated. You can't win the race in selling
unless you run on the track."* The ideal candidate for self-starting
success is the sales rep who has learned well a set procedure for
making sales.

While visiting the plant of a large, midwestern publishing firm, we
observed the many sales training courses, books and sales aids
which were laid out on display. Someone asked, "How did you
people ever prepare so much material?" The President laughed and
explained, "If it weren't for deadlines, we wouldn't need much
space." Deadlines are drivers. No matter how much you may
sometimes despise them, deadlines can be profitable to you. They
motivate you in making things happen now.

Florence Taylor expressed it well:

> *"Success is the sum of small efforts,*
> *Repeated day in and day out,*
> *With never a thought of frustration,*
> *With never a moment of doubt,*
> *Whatever your cherished ambition,*
> *Begin now to make it come true*
> *Through efforts, repeated, untiring,*
> *Plus faith in the thing you do!"*

The call goes out "Wanted: More Self-Starters." If you meet the
call, you will grow and go on to greater and higher levels of production in selling.

Positioning Precept
Be A Self-Starter

Put Off Procrastinating

*Procrastination is caused by our perception that doing
a certain task will cause us pain. We tend to avoid
events which are unpleasant, complex, lengthy,
or uninteresting, regardless of their priority.*

-Dr. John C. Maxwell

Do you have the tendency to procrastinate? If you do, you have fallen into the habit of putting off until tomorrow the jobs you previously put off until today. You are a person who has mastered the art of keeping up with yesterday.

You need to take a good, hard, honest, daily look at yourself to determine if you have slipped into the habit of putting things off until tomorrow — that never, never land where success is non-existent.

Write it on your heart: *Success is the product of today, of today's responsibilities fulfilled, of today's opportunities seized, of today's jobs attended to, of today's sales finalized.*

Tomorrow never really comes. Every morning when the sun rises, it's *today!* That's when the sales are made. That's when the all-important signatures are written on the dotted line.

Promise yourself *today* your work will be done *today*. Promise yourself *today* the unpleasant tasks will be cleared up *today*. Convince yourself *today* you owe it to yourself, your family and your organization to break loose from the bonds of procrastination and leap out into the exciting world to *today's* accomplishments, *present* achievements, and *immediate* rewards.

Do you ever promise yourself that tomorrow will be better? It *can* be, too, simply by making *today* the best day possible. To make tomorrow a great day, start *today!* Don't be like Mark Twain. He said, *"Never put off 'til tomorrow what you can do the day after tomorrow."*

There's a wise old saying that ought to haunt every salesperson, *"One of these days is none of these days."* Some sales reps get ready and then do something. Many just keep getting ready!

The interesting thing about "later" is it can never be proven false. One can never challenge or be critical of us. When confronted, we can always say, "I said I would do it later — and it's not later yet!"

In this manner, we can put off and delay indefinitely. Actually, we only run out of laters when we run out of breath. *Death is nature's way of saying, "No more laters left."*

One of the most valuable gifts you can give to yourself is to memorize — and to start each day by affirming — the lines of ancient wisdom translated from the Sanskrit:

> *"Listen to the exhortation of the dawn.*
> *Look well to this day! For it is life,*
> > *The very life of life.*
> *In its brief course lie all the verities*
> *And realities of your existence:*
> > *The bliss of growth,*
> > *The glory of action,*
> > *The splendor of beauty;*
> *For yesterday is but a dream,*
> *And tomorrow is only a vision,*
> > *But today well lived*
> *Makes every yesterday a dream of happiness*
> *And every tomorrow a vision of hope.*
> > *Look well, therefore, to this day!*
> > *Such is the salutation of the dawn."*

Remember, the hardest way to get any job done is to put it off. In the long run, the easiest way to get it done is to *do it now* and get it behind you. Bruce Springsteen expressed it well when he said, *"Stop waiting to become the person you want to be someday, and start living as that person today."*

Positioning Precept
Put Off Procrastinating

Believe In The Law Of Averages

*One of the great freedoms we have in the United States — one we
too often overlook —is the freedom to fail. Think about that for a
moment. It is an important freedom. It means we can
stick our chins out; we can play the percentages.
And we get the rewards from doing so.*

-Ray Eppert

Professionals are good at what they do, and they know why they
are good. Because they know why they are good, they critique
their own performances and naturally continue to grow and to
become better. These types of performance reviews show them
how to grow and become more effective.

Another characteristic of professionals is that they demonstrate a
strong belief in the law of averages. Knowing the numbers permits
them to have an almost total indifference to whether or not a given
prospect buys or not. One time, we saw a show on Broadway,
"Ben Franklin in Paris," starring Robert Preston. In this show,
Preston, playing the part of Franklin, said, *"When you are turned
down is simply the place where you begin to negotiate."* What a
valuable lesson to learn when you are in sales.

*When you meet resistance anywhere along the selling process,
that's the point where you begin to negotiate.* You'll get resistance
along the line. This isn't unique to selling. It's part of everything
in life that involves any element of competition.

Certainly, it's true in baseball. One year, late in the season,
Harmon Killebrew struck out for the 142nd time. That was a new
all-time major league record for strike-outs in a single season.
However, on the same day, Killebrew hit his 48th home run. That,
too, was a new all-time record for the most home runs ever hit by a

Minnesota Twins' player. Killebrew's unshakable faith in making the law of averages work for him enabled him to become one of baseball's all-time great sluggers. *In baseball, like selling, it all goes together. The most strikeouts, the most home runs.* Whatever it is you are selling, each disappointment, any delay, every turndown is like a strikeout. The important thing is to be a student of your business so you know the number of strikeouts you have had since your last hit. The greater the number, the nearer you are to your next hit!

Why do so few salespeople succeed big at a time when unusual success is available to everyone. Reflect upon our earlier discussion of The Common Denominator of success. Remember, Albert E. N. Gray's discovery — *"If you would succeed in selling, you must form the habit of doing what failures don't like to do."* We've discovered the thing failures dislike to do most is expose themselves to a large number of negative responses. *"Successful salespeople,"* Mr. Gray went on to say, *"are motivated by the desire for pleasing results. Failures are influenced by pleasing methods. They are inclined to be satisfied with such results as can be obtained by taking fewer turn-downs."*

The best-kept secret for obeying the law of averages and conquering selling fears and call reluctance lies in remembering your selling successes, however small. Erase from memory your failures, however large. Put this up on the mirror where you can digest it each day. Carry it with you on a 3x5 card. Remember it always. When this secret is learned, emotionally as well as intellectually, you'll begin putting your feet where the sales rep's feet always belong — on the road to another prospect.

We believe the "acid test" of your value as a sales rep is your response to the uninspired moments when you must demonstrate your belief in the law of averages.

You earn your success diploma in selling by realizing it's always too soon to quit. That's why you should always get up when you fall down!

Positioning Precept
Believe In The Law Of Averages

Make Habit Your Servant

The chains of habit are generally too small to be felt until they are too strong to be broken.

- Samuel Johnson

Psychologists tell us that we are governed by habit. They say every salesperson develops habits of thought and action that are good or bad, efficient or inefficient, regular or spasmodic. Dryden said, *"We first make our habits, and then our habits make us."* This is especially true relative to your career in selling. Your habits determine your behavior, your selling style and the way in which you spend your time. It's obvious you can attain consistent success only if you consciously develop habits that are sound, efficient and regular.

Dr. Richard Buskirk, Professor of Marketing at the University of Colorado, made an incisive observation when he said, *"Salespeople are successful more because of their philosophies, attitudes and habits than because of any special selling techniques they have learned. The mere possession of selling techniques does little to ensure your success. It's your attitudes and habits that make all the difference."* A salesperson is a bundle of habits. Your entire career will be given to forming, unforming and reforming habits.

If you are relatively new in the sales field, it's important to remember that it's as easy at this stage to develop good habits as bad. Mel H. Gregory, Jr., an outstanding marketing mind, says, *"There are four important habits every salesperson can and should develop at the start - punctuality, accuracy, simplicity and action."* He goes on to say, *"Punctuality saves you valuable time. Accuracy avoids costly mistakes. Simplicity helps you to be understood and more effective. Action makes it possible for you to take advantage of opportunities which, if lost, are impossible to recall."*

Perhaps you've been a sales rep for some time. Now, you find yourself plagued by poor habits. It will be encouraging for you to know that many successful sales reps one day awakened to a similar realization. Then, by careful planning, they jarred themselves out of the run of negative habits and went on to achieve outstanding success.

You can change! To develop a good habit, you must form a clear picture of the ideal result you seek to achieve. You must develop the capacity to substitute a new habit pattern while you are striving to overcome any bad habit. *Remember, habit is a quality that you must use positively to increase your selling effectiveness.*

Success in selling is something achieved by the minority. It is therefore unnatural and not to be achieved by following your natural likes and dislikes. Our experience while working in the field with hundreds of successful sales reps sold us on the wisdom of this statement, *"The chains of habit are generally too small to be felt until they are too strong to be broken!"*

> *I will push you onward or I'll drag you down to*
> *failure. I'm at your command.*
> *Half the tasks you do, you might just as well*
> *turn over to me. I'll do them quickly and correctly.*
> *I am easily managed. You must merely be firm*
> *with me. Show me exactly how you want*
> *something done and after a few lessons, I*
> *will do it automatically.*
> *I am the sermon of all great people, and a lash of all*
> *failures, as well. Those who are great, I*
> *have made great. Those who are failures,*
> *I've made failures.*
> *I'm not a machine, but I work with all the precision*
> *of a machine, plus the intelligence of a person.*

You may run me for profit or run me for ruin. The
        choice is yours. It makes no difference to me.
Take me, train me and be firm with me, and I'll lay
            your work at your feet. But be easy with
            me, and I will destroy you.
Who am I? Habit is my name!

Positioning Precept
Make Habit Your Servant

Manage Selling Time

*It's no good being a model of split-second efficiency
if you're working on the wrong things. A well-organized
person reviews the calendar as well as the clock.*

-Mark McCormack

In selling, you are always measured and rewarded by what you put into the hours, not by the hours you put in. Making good on your purpose in business and in life boils down to the way in which you invest your time. If you live to be 90 years old, you will have lived only 32,850 days. Each of those days, therefore, is a precious fragment of a gift called time — your time. It only makes sense to use every day well. Today is yours. Use it well.

Kerby Anderson, the well-known author and lecturer at Probe International writes, *"It has, perhaps, always been true that 'time is money.' But for the current generation, this maxim has a new twist. In the frenetic age in which we live, time has become even more scarce than money — and therefore more valuable."*

Del Smith, the highly successful CEO of Evergreen International Aviation, Inc., says this, *"I've become convinced that time is the most important factor in human existence. What you do with this precious commodity determines the course of your life. Each minute appears only once in all eternity. If not utilized, it's lost forever."*

Jack Parr, a well-known sales consultant from Salina, Kansas, expresses it this way, *"If you view the subject of time management only in terms of efficiency — only as guidelines for increasing the number of activities you can pack into a day, you have reason to be repelled by it. If you view it in terms of effectiveness — in terms of disciplines for eliminating unnecessary activities from your busy*

71

schedule to make way for satisfying, goal-directed activities, time management will be attractive to you." To increase your sales production and income, you probably won't need to work any harder — but you may need to work smarter.

One of the most underrated truths about selling is that unusual success follows the individual who identifies the vital factors that make a significant difference in producing results. This individual then focuses attention on those key, vital factors most of the time. *That's what Jack Parr means by being effective. The effective salesperson spends time on the high-payoff activities.*

To shape the kind of effective approach described by Parr, you'll find it helpful to view your business activities as being either "green" (vital), "yellow" (important), or "red" (tension-relieving).

Your green-time activities are setting appointments and making sales presentations. Yellow time includes planning, prospecting, studying, preparing, dictating, filing, etc. Each of these yellow activities may be necessary and important. However, improving or doing more of them is no guarantee of an improvement in production.

Red-time activities include drinking coffee and having a lengthy discussion of last night's ball game. It's an extended luncheon with someone who will never be a customer. These and others you can think of are tension-relieving activities.

Clearly, you have high-quality time and low-quality time. Green, yellow, and red activities all keep you busy, but they have strikingly different impacts on your "bottom line." *Remember, you are paid for results produced - not for the amount of time you put in. Never confuse activity with accomplishment.*

Like most success factors in selling, time management is largely dependent upon attitude. Develop your awareness of time and the manner in which you use it. Again, time is one of the major resources to utilize if you are to achieve outstanding success in selling.

Make it a practice to ask yourself, "What should I be doing with my time right now? What is it that really needs doing now? Am I staying in the green?" Place greater emphasis on <u>what</u> you do each day than on <u>how much</u> you do. Stay in the "green."

More than anything else, your attitude determines your success in managing time. Here are some key time-management, attitude-building thoughts to review regularly:

Define the "ideal day." This serves to reinforce discipline. It eliminates decisions on what to do next and ensures the scheduling of key activities.

When you start something, be determined to do it right the first time and bring it to a finish. The old cliché, "If you don't have time to do it right, when will you have time to do it over?" applies today, too. Resist the temptation to leave a job unfinished. It takes more time to refamiliarize yourself with a project than to complete it the first time around.

Become clock-conscious. Set your watch five minutes fast. It will make you time-conscious and keep you punctual.

Keep your written, daily plan visible. It's one good way to rout procrastination.

Earn a reputation for being busy. Others will show more respect for your time.

Establish deadlines with plans you make. Set time limits for doing certain jobs. You may have an hour to do a job, but don't take that hour for a 30-minute job.

Schedule breakfast and luncheon appointments. You'll discover "working meals" to be time-savers.

Have your secretary confirm appointments. This saves time by improving your "batting average" on appointments kept.

Schedule personal visits to doctors or dentists only when you can be their first patient of the day. Many professionals don't value their patients' time as they do their own.

Make the most of your transition time. You can gain a remarkable amount of information and inspiration if you listen to cassettes during your "in-between" time. Turn your automobile into a learning center. Also, invest in a cellular telephone for your car. Roger Staubach tells us it's his single, best time-saver.

Beware of perfectionism. If you tend to be a perfectionist, keep in mind that even by your standards you need to do some jobs quickly and be done with them. For perfectionists, preparation often becomes procrastination.

Develop your secretary as an assistant. In addition to handling routine correspondence, answering the telephone, and monitoring visitors and appointments, a secretary can be invaluable in anticipating needs and following up on handling details.

Skim books and magazines for ideas. Learn to skip over unnecessary details and omit copy that's only marginally informative. Take a speed-reading course. Retain usable ideas and quotations on 3 x 5 index cards.

Handle each piece of mail once. Frequently, a reply to letters can be made on the same sheet of correspondence. Save trivia to be handled once a week.

Decide which responsibilities you must be directly involved in and which ones can be delegated. Be sure to delegate effectively. "Dump and run" is generally a time-waster.

Plan unavailability. Plan a "quiet hour" each day for concentration and creative thinking. It will pay dividends.

Time management is a lifetime activity. To become good at it, you must have correct attitudes, workable strategies, and most of all, an adequate amount of self-discipline.

When your selling day is done, make one more call. We saved this one for last to make the point that managing time requires disciplining yourself to do things automatically. We've taught this one for years. However, it was Mark McCormack who brought it to mind again in one of his recent Success Secrets newsletters. Here's what he said, *"When you're through for the day, snapping your briefcase shut, turning off your computer and putting on your coat — always place one more call. This will strengthen your self-discipline and impact your checking account."*

Positioning Precept
Manage Selling Time

Form Self-Improvement Habit

You set your destiny by what you make of yourself.
Be an earnest student of yourself. Learn by frequent
self-examination to appraise and to improve
your attitudes, aspirations and habits.

-Grenville Kleiser

Someone once said that the biggest room in the world is the room for self-improvement. The effective salesperson is constantly improving in every area. We realize becoming a standout performer, as a rule, is not a "short haul" proposition. Building an outstanding career in selling is a long-term operation. As time passes, you should be capitalizing on past efforts. When an archer misses a mark, he or she turns and looks for the fault. *Failure to hit the bull's eye is never the fault of the target. Like the archer, to improve your aim, you must improve yourself.*

You must be willing to pay a price for self-improvement.

Greatness in selling is never something conferred, it's something achieved. It's not something given, it's something earned. It's not an accident of birth, it's an attitude of quality; a dimension, an outlook, a way of life that is open to anyone who is willing to pay the price. Channing Pollock once wrote, *"We should be content with what we have but never with what we are. The man who regards himself as a finished job is finished."*

Everyone is interested in improving. They want to improve their spouses. They want to improve their children. They want to improve their company, their country. Most of us want to improve everyone and everything. In the process, we neglect to improve the one person we can most readily and quickly impact — and that's ourselves. We are willing to change jobs, locations and industries. *Only rarely, do we change ourselves.*

All personal development in the long run is just that — personal. All development is self-development. It's easier to play ball with a perennial winner than it is to play with a team at the league's bottom. All athletes will tell you that you'll earn more, you'll get more recognition, get better coaching, have more fun and literally play better ball. To be a winner, to play on a winning team in the sales field, you must be constantly increasing your sales knowledge and improving your skills and strategies.

Keep thinking about being better and doing better. Keep planning for self-improvement. Remember, what we regularly and consistently affirm within ourselves, about ourselves and to ourselves, has a way of becoming reality. What is talent but originality robed in resourcefulness? What is achievement but a dream dressed in work clothes? What is accomplishment but ability stripped of its doubts? What is life but a series of opportunities masked as difficulties? *What is success but effort draped in day-to-day self-improvement.*

Lose yourself in productive, creative and necessary sales activities and you'll improve and enhance your selling achievements. This is your responsibility, your duty and your job. It's forming the self-improvement habit!

> *There's no thrill in easy sailing*
> > *When the skies are clear and blue.*
> *There's no joy in merely doing things*
> > *Which anyone can do.*
> *But there is some satisfaction*
> > *That is mighty sweet to take;*
> *When you reach a destination*
> > *That you thought you couldn't make.*

Positioning Precept
Form Self-Improvement Habit

Put Forth Honest, Intelligent Effort

*The highest reward for your toil is not what
you get for it, but what you become by it.*

-John Ruskin

Between the person you are and the person you'd like to be lies
your constant struggle.

*Have you observed that successful salespeople are doers? They
are not always as long on technical knowledge as they are in
motivating themselves to do what gets the job done.* They believe
a good start is a journey half completed, so they start and keep
going. They have the will power or determination to overcome
inertia. They are self-starters and self-promoters.

An honest day's work is our moral obligation. It's an obligation to
the company we represent, our families and ourselves.

What is an honest day's work? Who can say? The answer probably lies in our own conscience.

Just before you go to sleep, at the end of the day, if you can say,
*"Today I have given an effective, full day's effort to my selling job.
I have displayed discipline in planning, time management and
selling."* Perhaps this is the best answer to what is an honest day's
work.

The days have a way of slipping by almost before you can use
them. Successful people don't operate as if they have a patent on
time. Since a sales career is shorter than the blink of any eye, it's
no wonder the professionals handle their time with tender loving
care. With Benjamin Franklin, they are likely to agree, *"Dost thou
love life? Then do not squander time, for that's the stuff life is
made of."*

During your selling career, you'll only spend about 10 years earning a living. Ten years out of an entire lifetime is quite a bargain. You'll be asleep almost twice as long. Do you know that 30 minutes a day is equal to 22 full days a year? Just 30 minutes a day picked up between appointments, waiting for the train or driving to an appointment will increase your year by six percent when profitably used. This "in-between" time can contribute substantially to your effectiveness and fulfillment as a professional salesperson.

Recognize that spare moments are money. Don't throw them away any more than you would toss away a $50 bill. The primary attitude you want to develop is "time-sense."

When you put a dental appointment, a business meeting or a special event on your plan pad, as a rule you keep it. Do exactly the same with the things you want to accomplish with your in-between time. As a consequence, you'll find your spare moments becoming far more productive.

For example, well thought-out, well prepared daily work schedules can be completed during this time. Spend at least 10 minutes every day making out a "must do" list for the following day. Learn to use portable dictation equipment. You can use this to answer correspondence, prepare sales presentations and to instruct your secretary on appointments and items you'd like her to handle.

As a time-conscious salesperson, you'll learn to improve your personal efficiency by formulating your own methods and procedures. Develop the habit of having several quarters with you all the time so that calls can be made and returned in spare moments. Also, you will find it a practical procedure to carry postal cards prepared with your return address for writing short messages.

Certainly, you'll want to schedule reading on a regular basis. Listening to audio cassettes while you travel is an effective way to learn a wide range of subject matter.

The difference between what you actually accomplish, the selling rewards you actually generate, and the things you might accomplish, lies pretty much in the way you use your spare moments. Life itself can't give you joy, unless you really will it. Life just gives you space and time, it's up to you to fill it!

As Richmond said, *"There is a time to be born, and a time to die, but there is an interval between these two times of infinite importance."*

Positioning Precept
Put Forth Honest, Intelligent Effort

Do It — And Then Some!

*Our business in life is not to get ahead of others but to
get ahead of ourselves - to break our own records, to
out-strip our yesterdays by our today; to do the little
parts of our work with more force than ever before.*

-Stewart Johnson

Emmitt Smith, #22, is an All-Pro running back for the World
Champion Dallas Cowboys. His impressive statistics are well
known to football fans. Regularly, Emmitt leads all rushers in
yardage gained, yards per carry and touchdowns scored.

Little known and seldom talked about is what the football experts,
like John Madden, call Emmitt's most impressive statistic. *It's his
YAC numbers. That's correct — his Yards After Contact.* You
see, Emmitt is one of those "And then some" performers. He's at
his best after the initial resistance. *Emmitt is a model of excellence
on this score for everyone in selling to emulate.*

We're convinced those three little words — And Then Some —
make the difference between average salespeople and top performers.

Long before the famous discovery of Alexander Graham Bell,
Wilhelm Reiss, the German schoolmaster, constructed a telephone
through which he could whistle or hum. However, the gadget
couldn't transmit speech. Something was lacking! Reiss never let
the electrodes touch in his telephone. Bell then followed Reiss and
discovered that a little screw controlled the telephone electrodes.
Accidentally, he moved the screw one-thousandth of an inch and
speech, articulate and clear, came through. History records that the
fraction of an inch made an enormous difference.

You may be just that short distance from success in your selling career. Just a little improvement in your daily planning, a little adjustment in your sales presentation, a little additional product knowledge, a little more positive action, or persistence — and unusual success can become yours. *Plan and prepare purposefully, proceed positively, pursue persistently.*

Chances are good a very slight improvement in your day-to-day selling habits will have a huge cumulative impact at the end of your year. *"It is but the littleness of man that sees no greatness in trifles,"* said Wendell Phillips. Every selling day is a little life. Your entire selling life is but a day repeated. *Little random acts of kindness and courtesy can become your unique competitive edge.*

Gates of achievement swing wide for the salesperson who sees infinite possibilities in the insignificant. This is especially true with those sales reps who are determined to deliver a little extra and do a little extra. Consider three little words. They will point you toward success. The three words are — And Then Some.

We're convinced these words make the difference between average salespeople and top performers.

The high achievers do what is expected ...
And Then Some.

They hold themselves responsible for
higher standards. They make good
on commitments and responsibilities ...
And Then Some.

They can be counted on to represent
the company and themselves
in a professional manner. Their selling success secret
is wrapped up in these little words ...
And Then Some!

Positioning Precept
Do It — And Then Some

Precept Supporting Philosophies

The vitality of thought is an adventure. Ideas won't keep. Something must be done about them.
> — Alfred North Whitehead

You can't learn anything from experiences you're not having.
> — Louis L'Amour

We are what we repeatedly do.
> — Aristotle

When we do what we have always done, we get what we have always gotten.
> — Dr. Gerald Sentell

Spectacular results come from unspectacular preparation.
> — Roger Staubach

Honest, intelligent effort is always rewarded.
> — The Kinders

Habit is a cable; we weave a thread of it each day, and at last we cannot break it.
> — Horace Mann

All things are possible when ...
- I get organized to succeed.
- I get smarter people to help me.
- I get my ego out of the way.
- I'm willing to share the credit.
> — Robert Schuller

You don't concentrate on risks. You concentrate on results. No risk is too great to prevent the necessary job from getting done.
> — Chuck Yeager

Work is life and good work is good life.
> — James Elliott

Off The Professionals' Bookshelf

Covey, Stephen. *The Seven Habits Of Highly Effective People.* Simon & Schuster, 1989.

Lakein, Alan. *How to Get Control of Your Time.* NAL, 1973.

Mackay, Harvey. *Swim With The Sharks Without Being Eaten Alive.* Morrow, 1988

McCay, James. *The Management Of Time.* Prentice-Hall, 1959.

McCormick, Mark. *What They Don't Teach You At The Harvard Business School.* Bantam, 1984.

Mescon, Mike. *Showing Up For Work.* Peachtree.

Ringer, Robert. *Million Dollar Habits.* Wynwood Press, 1990.

Section Three
Selling Skill Developers

Your Company can spread its name widely through advertisement. It can employ talented people to support your selling efforts. It can provide superior products and services.

However, the average customer who buys these products and services will usually form his or her judgment of the Company through the contact made with a single sales rep. If that individual is poorly mannered, disorganized or inefficient, it will take a lot of doing and cultivating to overcome the first negative impression. Every person who, in any capacity, comes in contact with the buying public is a salesperson. The impression he or she makes is the Company's strongest advertisement, good or bad.

Selling is a challenge for everyone — and success in selling is always an Equal Opportunity Employer.

Give It Your Best

*The secret of success is to do the
common jobs uncommonly well.*

- John D. Rockefeller, Jr.

The motto of a prominent Chicago advertising agency reads,
"Where only the best is good enough." What a motto for life this
would be for you as a professional sales rep. Adopt it as yours.
Hang it up on your bedroom wall and display it in your office.
Carry it with you in your billfold. Weave it into the texture of
everything you do and your sales work is sure to become what you
want it to be — a masterpiece.

There is an indescribable superiority added to the character and
fiber of the sales people who consciously put the trademark of
quality on their work. The mental and moral effect of doing things
accurately, painstakingly and thoroughly, can hardly be estimated
because the processes are so gradual, so subtle. *Every time you
obey the inward law of doing right you hear an inward approval.*
On the contrary, every half completed, careless, slipshod job that
goes out of your hands leaves its trace of demoralization behind
and excellence becomes impossible. You'll like yourself much
better when you have the approval of your conscience.

There is no other advertisement for the professional sales rep like a
good reputation. Many of America's greatest manufacturers have
regarded their reputation as their most precious possession, and
under no circumstances would they allow their names to be put on
an imperfect article. *Large sums of money are often paid for the
use of a name because of its reputation for integrity, reliability,
and excellence.*

There is nothing like being enamored of excellence, being grounded with quality of service, as a selling principle. No other characteristic makes such a strong, lasting impression upon your customers. Never be satisfied with "fairly good," "pretty good," or "that's going to be O.K., I think." Do every selling job to a finish and accept nothing but your best every time. *Someone is watching. Someone will notice. And that someone can become a valuable customer.*

In Italy, during the early part of the Eighteenth Century, Stradivari put his stamp of excellence on the violins he "made for eternity." His workmanship was superior. Not one of his violins was ever known to break. *Stradivari did not need any patent on his violins, for no other violin maker would pay his price for excellence.* Every "Stradivarius" in existence today is still worth thousands of dollars.

As a sales rep, you can make your own "Stradivarius." Every bit of your work, no matter how unimportant or trivial it may seem, can bear your personal trademark of excellence. A top compensation expert, Robert Sibson, as reported in *Dun's Review,* says that this is a happy generation to have been born into. *This is particularly true for the professional salesperson dedicated and determined to make their own "Stradivarius." Never has the demand for them been higher, or the supply lower.*

There is great power in holding a high ideal of your sales work, for whatever model the mind holds, the life-style copies. Selling as a way of life teaches many lessons. One of the most important is that you are not paid for who you know — nor for what you know. As a professional salesperson, you're paid for the quality of service you provide with what you know, for those you know.

The greatest and perhaps the only perfect gift we can give to the world is the gift of ourselves at our best.

Bill Humphrey, the Senior Vice President of Marketing for Paul Revere, has this moving poem on his desk at his Worcester office.

Excellence

Excellence is dedication
To a job that's hard to do;
Going the extra mile —
Always following through.

Excellence is communication.
Sharing everything you know,
And learning how to listen
So your expertise will grow.

Excellence is appreciation
Of the talent that you see.
Acknowledging a job well done
Inspires success and loyalty.

Excellence is aspiration
With a higher goal in mind,
To trust in God and search for things
Of a more rewarding kind.

Jill Wolf

Positioning Precept
Give It Your Best

Look Like A Winner

Most all accomplishments in selling are preceded by an image of success. The proper image impresses others and can be a powerful motivating force for you.

-Melody Jaisson

Make certain you look like a success and you'll have something going for you the minute you get in front of prospects. You'll look as if you represent a reliable company. *You'll look as if you're accustomed to influencing people and closing sales.*

You can't very well make over your physical body or certain aspects of your appearance. However, you can do much to make the best of what you are. You can look successful. You can dress appropriately and wear your clothes neatly. People are more apt to like and, consequently, buy from those who appear neat, clean and successful. *Not only is appearance important because of the impression it makes on others, but also because of the psychological effect it has on you.*

"The way we dress has a remarkable effect on the people we meet. It greatly affects how they treat us," says John Malloy in *Dress For Success.*

It's for this reason that you want to check yourself regularly —

- Is my hair clean, trimmed, combed and styled for my face?

- Is my suit or dress pressed?

- Are the pocket flaps of my coat out?

- Are my hands clean? Nails trimmed and clean?

- Are there any aspects in my appearance that are distracting or which might prejudice a prospect?

These are important aspects of appearance. It's within your power to make sure you measure up on all of these counts.

Perhaps you recall seeing a cartoon picturing a tramp saying, "I'd give a thousand dollars to be one of them there millionaires." That sign always draws a chuckle. The amazing thing is, there are many people in sales who are much like that tramp. They would be willing to "give a thousand dollars" worth of attention to their personal appearance, in exchange for a million dollars in sales results.

You can learn to give the impression of success and confidence. By doing so, you'll automatically increase your chances for having a more receptive interview. The usual prospect reaction becomes, "This sales rep must have a good product or service and I ought to listen to him." All it takes is careful attention to a few simple details.

From every point of view, it pays well to dress well. Always look neat and well-groomed. The knowledge that you are handsomely dressed, have well-groomed hair and clean, manicured fingernails, will act as a mental tonic. Proper balance in dress, with well-shined shoes, is important too.

William I. O'Donnell, a past president of the insurance industry's prestigious Million Dollar Round Table, offers these basics for presenting a professional image:

- *Purchase better clothing (spend twice as much; buy half as many).*
- *Always be well groomed. Dirty hair, nails, and shoes are a turn-off.*
- *You never have to apologize for overdressing. Just slip off your coat or loosen your tie.*

- *Know how the people to whom you are selling dress, and dress at least as well as they do or like they dress.*
- *Gaudy jewelry does not impress, it distracts. Cheap or sport jewelry diminish the value of an expensive wardrobe.*
- *A good pen and pencil set are more admired than the drugstore special.*
- *An expensive tie will increase the perceptive value of a less expensive suit.*
- *Maintain your authority by wearing your suit coat. If the senior decision maker in the meeting removes his jacket, you can remove yours.*
- *Shined shoes improve your respectability and credibility.*
- *Take a couple of extra minutes to review your outfit before you leave home in the morning.*

Remember, too, the importance of nutrition, exercise and proper rest. You can't store physical fitness. You must work to maintain it daily. *The salesperson with a high level of energy has a definite competitive edge.* Make certain you achieve and maintain that edge.

If you wear glasses, remember the shape of the lenses and color of the frames will greatly affect your general appearance.

Nothing succeeds like success. Observe the successful salespeople you know. In most cases, can't you tell they are successful just by looking at them? Yes, the business world accepts the Shakespearean truth, *"the apparel oft proclaims the man."*

If you look like a winner, it's much easier to be one. *That's true, and it's also true that the winners in selling are always the best paid!*

Positioning Precept
Look Like A Winner

Enjoy Every Sales Call

*We are what we are because of what
we do with our opportunities.*

-Ron Price

What a difference it could make in your sales career and in the lives of your prospects and customers if you made a discovery of an immense reserve of power and energy within yourself. *Your enthusiasm might be as if you discovered oil in your backyard.*

Every salesperson who reads these words actually has a huge, hidden reservoir of power and energy. You have it. We have it. All of us have it. *It's like a vast pool of underground oil, waiting in silence and darkness for someone to discover it.*

Seldom will this hidden power of yours, or the pool of oil, reveal its presence by "seeping to the surface." *It has to be discovered by a disciplined effort.*

There is one interesting, striking difference. *Every barrel of oil pumped from a pool leaves that much less — while every time you use your hidden power in a selling situation, it becomes that much stronger the next time around.*

Imagine a heavy plank lying on the ground. Let's say it's two feet wide, five inches thick, and ten yards long. Confidently, you could race across the full length of this plank, turn around at the end, and race back. You could do it a hundred times.

Let's position this same plank rigidly between the roofs of two high skyscrapers. There's several hundred feet of empty space below. There's always the possibility you might be able to motivate yourself to cross it — but your feelings would be strikingly different!

Reason and logic tell you that you can successfully run across the plank. You could do it a hundred times on the ground. It's strong and sturdy. It won't spring or sway. *Will all of that reason and logic change your feelings about running across that plank high in the air?*

Reason and logic tell you there is nothing to dread about making the next call. But your subconscious mind rejects reason and logic like a sponge rejects coarse gravel. *It absorbs imagination — thirstily!* Nothing can keep your subconscious from responding. When you feed it the right things, it will absorb them. *It must respond. Therefore, the whole key to enjoying every sales call is to give your subconscious something useful to absorb.*

One of the best illustrations of how quickly and positively the subconscious responds is to be found in this well-known fact about selling. *The best time to make a new call is right after you have made a good sale. At that precise time, your attitude is perfect.*

By giving your subconscious something useful to "chew on and digest," you'll consistently create the same kind of attitude you have when you're "hot." You'll be able to neutralize the ineffective, purposeless feelings you have when you're "cold."

The strategy you use is quite simple. Before every sales call, ask yourself this question: *How would I feel about making this call if I knew it was going to be a good sale?*

Concentrate on the details. Imagine the relaxed, confident feeling you would have, the enthusiasm you would feel, the way you would walk and talk. *Imagine the command you would have of yourself and the situation.* Visualize all the details of how you would feel and act if the next call was guaranteed to be a good sale.

This is the entire formula. You don't need to complicate it. Don't try to reason it out. Just use it. It works! You'll be poised, confident and enthused. You'll never be tense, timid or tentative.

Do prospects respond to this kind of greeting? Use it and see!

Positioning Precept
Enjoy Every Sales Call

Pay Attention

*Michael Arden, a wonderful writer, said to me once that
the greatest act is to pay attention. That's so true.
I think the one lesson I've learned is that there is
no substitute for paying attention.*

-Diane Sawyer

At the end of a long and highly successful career, Tom Ferns in
Akron was asked for the most important advice he would give
Generation X individuals entering the selling profession. Tom said
this, *"Tell them to start early and stay late. Most of all, remind
them how important it is to pay attention."* This is the secret of
superior performers in selling — they keep their eyes open and
they ask questions of themselves and others.

It will not take you long to develop the habit of paying attention
and seize salient points. Decide to be a shrewd observer. All
things being equal, it is the keen observer who moves ahead. No
matter where you go, study the situation. Make important deduc-
tions from what you see and hear. Let nothing escape you. It will
be one of the greatest factors in your selling success.

Ruskin said, *"Hundreds of people can talk for one who can think;
but thousands can think for one who can see."* Most salespeople
don't see things; they merely look at them. They listen but do not
hear. *The power of keen observation is indicative of a superior
mentality.* "Paying attention" is a powerful mental process. It will
keep your mind on the material which the eyes and ears bring it —
considering, forming opinions, planning, estimating, weighing and
calculating.

"Paying attention" is a key to increasing your productivity. It
prompts you to learn as much as possible about your prospects —

their reputations and capacities, who they are buying from now and what they are receiving for their dollars.

"Paying attention" helps you do your homework and plan each call in advance. It makes it possible for you to evaluate carefully your prospects' problems and to decide upon the best solutions to help them. You'll learn to utilize sales aids and demonstration techniques which, in turn, reduce the number of time-consuming questions you will have to field. Finally, when you pay attention, you'll use your "in-between time" profitably. You'll confine your study, correspondence and report-writing to non-selling hours. When you find yourself with extra time, you'll build good will and discover a lot of useful prospecting information.

Before we leave this issue, let's be reminded of the power that comes to those professionals who pay attention to the following thoughts:

1. *Thou shalt have a goal powerful enough to withstand obstacles.*
2. *Thou shalt always believe in thyself.*
3. *Thou shalt keep holy this moment, for within it is the power of creation.*
4. *Thou shalt honor learning, persistence and simplicity.*
5. *Thou shalt light the way with enthusiasm.*
6. *Thou shalt strive with other builders.*
7. *Thou shalt give more than is expected.*
8. *Thou shalt be honest with thyself.*
9. *Thou shalt bring value to those ye serve.*
10. *Thou shalt find the best in every project.*

"What is it called?," asked a visitor in an art studio, as he was shown many sculptures. He had singled out a sculpture with winged feet and a face concealed by hair. "Opportunity," replied the sculptor. "Why is his face hidden?" the visitor asked. "Because men seldom know him when he comes to them." "Why does he have wings on his feet?" "Because he is soon gone and, once gone, cannot be overtaken."

The important sales information and insights you develop by paying attention — by keeping your eyes, ears and mind open — will assure you an enviable spot at the top of your company's sales honor roll.

Positioning Precept
Pay Attention

Listen To Learn

*Good listeners generally make
more sales than good talkers.*

-B. C. Holwick

Books have been written, courses have been developed and there is all kinds of material on how to be a more effective listener. Every salesperson should read and study all he or she can on this important area of selling.

- *By listening, you show prospects you respect their opinions.*

- *By listening, you show prospects you're really interested.*

- *By listening, you learn how to guide, direct and assist prospects.*

- *By listening, you help prospects help themselves.*

- *By listening, you exert subtle pressures on prospects.*

Many sales are consummated because the sales rep had the street smarts and the empathy to listen. By the same token, many sales are lost because the sales rep talked more than he listened.

If we could establish an axiom in this area, it would go something like this: Effective sales reps are good listeners.

Effective salespeople establish empathy with prospects by listening to what they have to say. Even though many sales are lost because the sales rep talked too much, we have never heard of an instance where a sale was lost because the sales rep listened too much.

Silence is a powerful selling strategy. When you employ silence, you give your prospects time to think. The only way they can think, the only way they can consider your recommendations, is for you to "punctuate" with some silence. Give them a chance to talk. Give them a chance to express their ideas or to ask a question.

The so-called experts estimate salespeople spend about 70 percent of their waking hours in some form of verbal communication. It breaks down this way: nine percent of their time is spent writing; 16 percent is spent reading; 30 percent is devoted to talking; and 45 percent, almost half the time we're awake, is spent listening. You can see why it is a good idea for you to develop listening skills.

Here are proven ways to increase your listening power:

Pay attention! This might seem too obvious to mention. However, it's surprising how many of us try to fake our attention. While listening to someone, we should look at them — squarely in the eye is always best — and give them the attention and respect we appreciate so much when we are talking.

Recognize the importance of skillful listening. If you don't accept the fact it's beneficial to hear more of what prospects say, there's no reason to bother improving this creative power.

Observe prospects' gestures and facial expressions. Empathy is one of the outstanding marks of a master salesperson.

Don't rule out any topic of discussion as totally uninteresting. Creative people are always on the lookout for new and different information. Keep your mind open for new ideas. Let your mind exercise itself as often as possible so that you can strengthen its capacity. This is just the same as exercising any muscle to avoid atrophy. New ideas are all around you and many of them will come by way of the spoken word. Absorb everything you can. You'll become better informed.

Avoid prejudging the speaker. Listen to what is said, the way it is said — and ask yourself why it is being said.

Become a note-taker. While listening, take notes which you can review later. This suggestion will help you jog your memory, and bring back major points and compliment your prospects in the process.

Listen for areas of mutual interest. Resist distraction. Remember, our minds can think at a speed of 500 words per minute, but prospects talk at about 125 words a minute.

When put into practice, these recommendations will help you listen better and learn more.

Positioning Precept
Listen To Learn

Be A Relationship Builder

People like doing business with those people they enjoy. They are more likely to make concessions to them. The bottom line is that you can get more of what you want by making prospects feel comfortable. When people like each other, the details rarely get in the way. When people don't like each other, details are likely to become insurmountable obstacles.

-James Henning

The well-known investor, Warren Buffett, has three qualifications for judging his investment opportunities. *He never invests with anyone he doesn't trust, respect and like — regardless of how good the numbers look.*

How many times have you heard it said, "When all things are equal, prospects have a strong tendency to buy from individuals they trust and like best." This is easily understood. *The interesting thing is this — in this age of relationship marketing, should things not be equal, prospects show the same tendency. Like Mr. Buffet, they still tend to buy from salespeople they trust, respect and like the most.*

As we move toward the 21st Century, the competitive edge will come to those sales reps who are effective relationship builders. *Relationship building is a learned skill.* It boils down to forming ten simple habits. Let's look at these crucial habits.

1)   **Use prospects' preferred names**. A very simple habit, but one you'll see violated often.

2)   **Show up on time**. Being punctual shows you care.

3) **Compliment appearances.** This indicates you're alert and paying attention.

4) **Make prospects look smart.** Build confidence in propects.

5) **Recognize achievements.** Sending congratulatory notes is a profitable use of time.

6) **Do something nice for some member of prospects' families.** This is a sure way to get close to your prospects.

7) **Point to possessions in which prospects have pride.** Again, this demonstrates you pay attention.

8) **Give prospects business.** Giving them leads or sending them information that might be helpful to them wins prospects over.

9) **Say "please" and "thank you."** These are always strong relationship builders.

10) **Do what you say you're going to do.** Treat commitments made as debts yet to be paid.

These ten simple habits may seem rather obvious. However, the failure to observe them is probably the single biggest cause of loss of credibility in relationships with others. As Jim Rohn said, *"One person caring about another represents life's greatest value."* Successful salespeople have successful habits; unsuccessful salespeople have unsuccessful habits. These ten habits are those you'll find possessed by successful salespeople.

To know the talented author and highly respected businessman, Bob Briner, has been one of life's richest blessings for us. Bob is a remarkable relationship-builder. Bob never stops working at staying in touch and strengthening relationships.

Here's an example of relationship-building at its best. We received a fax from Bob on Christmas Eve. After thanking us for a little gift we had sent him, Bob said, *"On this day of contemplating the greatest GIFT, I'm also mindful of the great gift of your friendship, mentoring and example of godliness. As I look forward to the New Year, I'm asking God to help me be a better friend to you and a more willing servant."*

That's a master salesman in action. You can't beat salespeople like that. You might manage to tie them occasionally — but you'll never beat them!

> *Can you say tonight in parting*
> *   with a sales day that's slipping fast,*
> *That you've helped one person*
> *   of the many you have passed?*
> *Is a single life rejoicing over something*
> *   you said or sold?*
> *Does one whose hopes were fading*
> *   now with courage look ahead?*
> *Did you waste the day or lose it, was it*
> *   well or poorly spent?*
> *Did you leave a trail of service*
> *   or a scar of discontent?*
> *As you close your eyes in slumber do you*
> *   think that God would say,*
> *You have made the world much better for the*
> *   relationships you made today.*

Author Unknown

Positioning Precept
Be A Relationship Builder

Prepare Logically - Adapt Needfully

Selling is a business of dips, dives, diversions,
changes, adaptations, and rolling with the punches.
If we know that, why not make these detours work
for us instead of destroying our energy?

-Burt Meisel, CLU

Someone said, "The trouble with life is you're halfway through before you realize it's one of those do-it-yourself deals."

Success in selling is much like that - it's another of those do-it-yourself deals. Consider the counsel of Dr. Alexis Carrel: *"The most effective way to live effectively is to make a plan of one's day every morning, and every night examine the results produced."*

Some of the most successful sales reps we know use a similar strategy. Before they close off the day's work, they spend high pay-off time writing down the specific things they plan to do the following day. They carefully plan tomorrow's sales activities. Their second step - one of equal importance - is that when tomorrow arrives they follow through and do the things they planned. *This kind of advance planning increases their effectiveness and sets them up for success. Their sales records prove it!*

Fred Smith, the high profile Dallas consultant, underscores the value of the "plan, then accomplish" practice. Fred writes, *"I like to have around me people who are excited about getting things done. I want the individuals who are flexible and who do not confuse flexibility with lack of integrity."* Consider what the great football coach, Tom Landry had to say: *"Only the individual who plans, prioritizes, and performs with positive action can find time for the important and the unexpected."*

Successful planning involves a degree of flexibility. *"Make big plans,"* Charley "Tremendous" Jones advises, *"but be willing to change your plans as the situation changes."* The situation is always the boss.

Study the word **PLAN**. To us, it's always meant: *Prepare Logically - Adapt Needfully.* In other words, make thoughtful, definite plans. Then, adapt and modify those plans as the situation might require.

Great salespeople, like effective performers in all walks of life, are those who are organized, flexible, and adaptable. *They size up situations and, when the occasion demands, they quickly, effectively and confidently alter their original course and go to "Plan B."* In the Navy, this kind of adaptability is referred to as changing the course.
 In the Boy Scout Woodbadge training, it's called improvising. In football, it's "calling an audible." *In selling, it's adapting the prepared agenda to meet the need.*

Roger Staubach, the Hall of Fame Quarterback, was a master of flexibility and adaptability. When his pass receivers were covered and there was no one to throw to, Roger knew what to do and how to do it. Quickly, he would pass the ball off to a secondary receiver, or he found some running room, followed his blocking, and picked up the necessary yardage. *After having Prepared Logically, he Adapted Needfully. Like the pro in selling, Roger understood that the situation becomes the boss!* Interestingly, Roger is still embracing the flexible planning habit as one of the top commercial real estate performers in the country.

You must learn to be the "quarterback" in every sales encounter. When the "defense" starts giving you the most trouble, in the form of objections and resistance, "call an audible." Adjust and adapt. Display flexibility. Move ahead to achieve your goal — another satisfied customer.

Positioning Precept
Prepare Logically - Adapt Needfully

Develop Call Courage

You'll always miss 100% of the shots you decide not to take.

- Wayne Gretsky

The World Insurance Group of a major financial institution sponsored a survey of Million Dollar Round Table members. The members were asked to rate a series of personal attributes relative to succeeding in selling. *The attribute ranked "Most Important" in this survey was self-confidence.* There are a lot of reasons for the lack of self-confidence and for call reluctance. And all of them get in the way of successful selling. Learning how to arm yourself against the self-defeating effect of negative encounters is a "must lesson" for anyone aiming for success in selling.

Whether or not you're conscious of it, you carry into every selling situation a rather definite picture of yourself. *The stronger your purpose and the belief in what you are selling, the more likely you are to project yourself as an intelligent, informed, competent professional.*

Right from the start, you want to eliminate timidness, hesitancy, and apology from your manner and speech. Here's something from Shakespeare that has helped us a lot over the years: *"Our doubts are traitors, and make us lose the good we oft might win by fearing to attempt."* And it was Goethe who said, *"Boldness has genius, power and magic in it."*

You'll learn to cope with call reluctance and to build call courage by following these suggestions:

- **Stay sold on what you are selling**.

- **Saturate your mind with positive, upbeat feelings.** Tell yourself you're enthusiastic and effective. You're prepared and persuasive. Take these "mental vitamins" regularly and you'll be able to trigger favorable responses.

- **Prepare yourself technically.** Know your product. Learn your lines. Prepare so that your presentations are as natural as your breathing. Knowing all about your ideas and learning your lines gives you a competitive edge. It builds your persuasion power — your call courage.

- **Focus on the rewards of success.** *Remember, your next call can result in a sale that can change your entire week or month — even your year or career.* Imagine how you'll feel after this kind of experience. You can control what you imagine. Feelings follow thought. Act the way you want to feel.

- **Remind yourself that most people are nice people.** Remember, prospects often fail to show they are nice during the early minutes of an initial contact. This is especially true of first-time buyers. New prospects are often tense and nervous and act a bit "abnormal" — as though they aren't too nice. This is an even stronger reason for you to stay in control and deport yourself as a poised, confident professional. *Let prospects key off of your attitude — never key off of theirs.*

- **Take the pledge.** Memorize the following pledge. Feed it into your mental computer and keep it on instant recall for the rest of your selling career.

I will never begin talking to a prospect on the telephone, in a seminar, or on an interview until I have written out my script, rehearsed and learned the lines so they can be expressed naturally, conversationally, and persuasively.

Taking this pledge will be a confidence builder for these reasons: First, you will say the right thing, consistently, not occasionally. Second, you'll tell your story in the fewest words. Third, it will give you more confidence because you know what you're going to say. Many successful sales reps owe their substantial production and earnings today to "taking the pledge."

Call courage must be developed if you are to succeed in selling. You must conquer call reluctance. As the late Dr. Maxwell Maltz, the distinguished plastic surgeon and author of *Psycho-Cybernetics,* always said, *"The surest way to develop courage is to act courageous. Do the thing you fear - and do it now!"* Call courage will follow.

Positioning Precept
Develop Call Courage

Choose Words Carefully

A word fitly spoken is like apples
of gold in pictures of silver.

-Proverbs 25:11

Communication — everyone is discussing it, studying it, practicing it. Yet, despite improved communication skills, you may feel like the sales rep who said to the prospect, *"I know you believe you understand what you think I said, but I am not sure you realize that what you heard is not what I meant."*

In selling, good communication involves more than good speaking. It also requires choosing the right words, the fewest words and the motivational-strength words.

In selling, your principal tools are words. Keep them razor sharp.

Napoleon wisely said, *"Thought is impossible without words. Rule people with words."* He might have added, "Rule each sales situation with the right words."

The salesperson who hopes to cut through the tough underbrush of sales resistance must have a ready supply of colorful, motivational-strength words and phrases at his or her command.

The right word, spoken with emphasis, enthusiasm, and expectancy, becomes your "laser beam" that can melt the granite-like objections of the toughest customer.

In selling, your principal tools are words. Keep them short!

Long, technical words often cause fences and walls to come between you and your prospects. Short, crisp words are far more likely to build bridges of understanding, goodwill and successful sales records. The talented communicator, Bill Gove, says the strongest words in selling may be these: *"I want to make certain I know how you feel."* Simple words, but words that sell because they communicate you care.

To interest your customers — to get them "leaning" your way — use words that probe and motivate. Avoid the words that irritate. Study the following words and expressions:

Words That Probe	*Words That Motivate*
Why?	Thank you
How?	Congratulations
What is your opinion?	Let's
What do you think?	I would appreciate your courtesy
Can you illustrate?	I want to make certain I understand
What do you consider?	I'm proud of you
What were the circumstances?	Please
How do you feel about ...?	Profit
Could you explain?	Guarantee
Which would be best for you?	

Words That Irritate

Understand?	Bucks
Get the point?	Deal
Do you see what I mean?	I, me, my, mine
To be honest with you	You know

John Donohue asks these thought-provoking questions of every salesperson who is interested in being better understood:

- Why use optimum instead of best?

- Why do we hear compensation but not salary?
- Why rationale instead of reason?
- Why utilization instead of use?
- And why implementation as today's replacement for start?

In selling, your principal tools are words. Be sure you gain under-standing.

"The finest words in the world, wrote Anatole France, *are only vain sounds, if you can't comprehend them."* In sales, you must be understood. Keep it simple.

Be sure your words mean exactly what you intend them to say. The word "bill" means one thing to a budget-conscious housewife. It means something else to a banker, and something entirely different to your Senator.

Unfortunately, you can't excuse your lack of communication as one parent tried to do when she told her young son, "Don't listen to what I say - listen to what I mean!"

Words, carefully chosen, properly used, and effectively spoken, can be the magic carpets on which you transport your products or services from the warehouse to your customer.

We remember being told one time that the five most powerful words in selling are:

"I am proud of you"

The four most powerful:

"What is your opinion?"

The three most powerful:

"May I ask ..."

And the two most powerful:

"Thank you!"

Words are the very heart of your sales presentation. Choose your words carefully. They will serve you well. You will gain understanding. You will be an effective communicator. Your sales will reflect it!

Positioning Precept
Choose Words Carefully

Maintain Enthusiasm

*People who are unable to motivate themselves
must be content with mediocrity,
no matter how impressive their other talents.*

-Andrew Carnegie

Enthusiasm is at the foundation of all progress! Talent is valuable but, without enthusiasm, it pales at the point of sale. Enthusiasm is the difference between mediocrity and superior success in selling.

Where do you get this energizing quality of enthusiasm? How do you maintain it after you tap into it? Two admonitions:

1)   *Take responsibility for your own level of enthusiasm throughout the selling day.*

2)   *Act as if you have enthusiasm even when you do not. Feelings always follow actions!*

In these two admonitions, you'll find a reservoir from which enthusiasm will flow and be sustained.

Admonition One: *Take responsibility for your own level of enthusiasm.* Don't leave it in the hands of others or with the circumstances around you. Learn what creates enthusiasm for you. Then, do it — turn it on!

What are your first thoughts when you start a new day? Do you remind yourself of the good news? That's the beginning of enthusiasm for that day.

I have a high level of energy.
That's good news!

I have a mind that is alert.
That's good news!

I have challenging work to do.
That's good news!

I have a strong market with great potential.
That's good news!

I'm creating my future today.
That's tremendous!

This kind of self-talk, used as your first thoughts for the day, begins the generation of enthusiasm. *Take responsibility for seeing that good news is identified and reflected upon.*

Dr. Harvey Cushing, a creative and imaginative writer, says, *"Enthusiasm is the fly-wheel which carries your saw through the knots in the log."* Your selling day will have knots in it. You'll need enthusiasm to get you through them.

Whose job is it to sustain a high level of contagious enthusiasm? Yours! No one sustains enthusiasm automatically. *It must be nourished with new vision, new goals, new commitments and new actions.*

Sustain your enthusiasm throughout the day by formulating new ideas from the reading of books, listening to audio cassettes, viewing video tapes. Nothing creates enthusiasm like imagination that has been set afire. Light the flame with new ideas. Enthusiasm will rise exponentially!

Admonition Two: *Act as if you have enthusiasm even when you don't.* Psychologists have concluded that it is easier to act your way into a new way of feeling than it is to feel your way into a new way of acting. Read that statement again. Think about it. It translates to this: *Act as if you feel enthusiastic and you will feel enthusiastic.*

William Shakespeare, the bard of English literature, challenges: *"Assume a virtue, if you have it not."* If you lack sustained enthusiasm, act as if you do have it. Don't spend your energy trying to feel enthusiastic. Act enthusiastic and enthusiasm will be yours!

Nothing great or new can be done without enthusiasm. A certain excessiveness always characterizes greatness. Enthusiasm is. reason gone mad to achieve a worthy ideal.

Enthusiasm reflects confidence, spreads good cheer, raises morale, inspires associates, and generates loyalties. It draws customers to you like a magnet. Enthusiasm, like measles, mumps, and the common cold, is highly contagious.

Take responsibility for sustaining your own enthusiasm throughout every day. Act as if you have enthusiasm even if you lack it. Let enthusiasm radiate from your voice. Let it be seen in your facial expressions. Let it be heard in the words you use. Use it to fill the thoughts you think.

You are never poor if you possess the emerald of enthusiasm. You are never rich without it.

Positioning Precept
Maintain Enthusiasm

Sell Courageously

Compared to what we ought to be, we are only half awake. The average individual performs far below potential. We possess power of various sorts which we habitually fail to use.

-William James

After Dr. David Livingstone had begun his now famous missionary work in Africa, a certain group wrote the great pioneer and asked: "Have you found a good road to where you are? If so, please advise. We'd like to send others to assist you."

Dr. Livingstone sent this reply: *"If you have those who will come only if they know there is a good road, I don't want them. I want individuals who are strong and courageous. Those who will come if there is no road at all!"*

What a lesson in courage — especially for salespeople.

A stranger asked an old-timer where the best fishing was in that area. Obligingly, the local authority on fishing holes replied: "You go down this road 'til you come to a big sign on a tree that says, 'No Trespassing.' You keep going! Then you come to a high fence with a sign that reads, 'Do Not Enter - Dangerous Bull Inside.' That's where you climb the fence! Then you walk about a mile and come to a bend in the creek where a big sign warns, 'Absolutely No Fishing. Trespassers Will be Prosecuted To The Full Extent Of The Law.' Mister, that's where you'll catch the biggest fish. Drop your line right there!"

An ancient proverb reminds us: *"Courage consists not so much in avoiding danger as in conquering it."*

Courage is performing the task that would be easier not to do. Courage is accepting the responsibilities when it would be more comfortable not to accept. It's moving out on faith, when you know full well the risks and the pitfalls that will challenge you. It's marching ahead, blazing a new trail where there are no roads - and sometimes no maps to guide you.

Courage is the quality that helps make professional sales people the highest-paid men and women in America.

Remember these truths:

"Courage is knowing what not to fear."
— Socrates.

"One man with courage makes a majority."
— Andrew Jackson

"To see what is right, and not to do it, is want of courage." — Confucius

"All problems become smaller if you don't dodge them but confront them. Touch a thistle timidly, and it pricks you; grasp it boldly, and its spines crumble."
— Wendell Halsey

"Whatever you do, you need courage. Whatever course you decide upon, there is always someone to tell you that you are wrong. There are always difficulties arising which tempt you to believe that your critics are right. To map out a course of action and follow it to an end, requires some of the same courage which a soldier needs. Peace has its victories, but it takes brave individuals to win them."
— Ralph Waldo Emerson

Years ago we read something about the rewards of courageous selling efforts. It was from a talk of W. J. Cameron, Vice President at Ford Motors in Detroit. We put it on a 3x5 card and refer to it often.

> *"What is needed for 1962 (or the 21st Century) is inspired, courageous sales effort. Men and women who will go to their selling jobs as a farmer goes to his plowing. He doesn't attend a preliminary 'pep session' in the farm kitchen to 'inspire' him for his work, he simply puts himself between the handles of his plow and plows — daily, doggedly, deliberately plodding and plugging along, not wondering about the 'future,' but steadily turning up the furrows. It's not a question of enthusiasm, it's a question of persistence based on knowledge that, if not now, then later, every investment of courageous effort will yield its return. We do not say that if you do this you will get results. We do say that those who do this are getting results."*

Positioning Precept
Sell Courageously

Sell Ethically

*Conduct your personal and professional life to set an
example that good, talented people admire and respect.*

-Bill Esrey

At the center of all you do in selling is all that you are. It's the
core issue. Ethics is not a discipline you learn. *Ethics is a statement of who you are.*

Ethics is a way of life that is intricately woven into your daily
selling activities. Your Code of Ethics is not a set of principles to
be framed and hung like a picture collecting dust on a wall.

A made-for-TV movie, "The Revolver," tells us the story of a
young man who stopped some thieves who were snatching a lady's
purse. Though he was a student and had no money, when the
woman tried to pay him a reward, he would not accept it. A friend
who had observed the entire incident asked why he wouldn't take
the money. His explanation was simple, *"There are some things
that you do for the soul."*

That's a marvelous description of what ethics is — something that
you do for the soul. It's doing the right thing because doing the
right thing is the right thing to do. That's ethical behavior.

Most of us learn ethical principles at home, in our schools or
through religious institutions. But there comes a time when those
principles must become a part of your daily selling behavior. They
must be lived out in our selling careers.

What is your ethical base? Can you articulate it? Can you identify how it influences your personal and professional behavior?

Dave Thomas, founder of Wendy's fast food stores, says that success begins inside. Unless your attitudes and beliefs are right, you can never be a real success in the world around you. He contends that people can never really have their act together unless three things are true about them: *They are honest, they believe in something, and they are self-disciplined.*

In his book, *Well Done*, Thomas communicates in down-to-earth language the ethical base for Wendy's. That's something you ought to be able to do.

As a professional in selling, ethics must include an awareness that you are a part of a larger society. It's a recognition that your life and your work are intertwined with the lives and works of many others. *Your behavior indelibly impacts the work of other people.*

Your recommendations do have a positive or a negative effect on the life of your clients. *Your dealings with the companies that provide your product line affect their bottom-line results and thereby the service they are able to provide for your customers.* Your behavior impacts your own reputation and business success. Your life is a part of many other lives.

A pebble dropped in a pond has an amazing effect on the entire ecology of the pond. Such is the influence of your behavior. The ripple effect is beyond measure. This kind of awareness is the beginning of ethical behavior.

Here are a few philosophies for selling ethically. You'll want to review these often and let them dominate your selling style.

- Efficiency is doing a thing right. Effectiveness is doing the right thing. First Class customer service requires both.

- Hold yourself responsible for higher standards than anyone else expects of you.

- Everyone has an invisible sign hanging from their neck that reads: "Make me feel important." Never forget this message when working with prospects and customers.

- Quality is the first thing seen. Service is the first thing felt. Price is the first thing forgotten.

- Always exceed the customer's expectations.

- Never let a customer problem go unresolved.

- A sales rep is essentially a teacher and advisor to the customer. The emphasis cannot be upon selling alone. Delivering Quality Service to the customer is the essential objective.

Maintaining high ethical standards is the right thing to do, and it's also good business. *A spotless reputation is an invaluable marketing asset.* Competency and trust comprise the framework for marketplace success. Build them every day with your commitment to excellence and by selling ethically.

Positioning Precept
Sell Ethically

Be A Generator

*If you're not building relationships or communicating
ideas, you may become a successful order taker, but
you'll never be a successful salesperson.*

-Charles H. Brower

Every organization has two types of sales reps — generators and
interceptors. Generators represent only 20 percent of the sales
force, but consistently produce 80 percent of the business.

Why is that? Well, if you study the generators, you'll discover
they have seven characteristics. Let's study these traits and decide
how they can become ours.

First, generators are well rehearsed. They invest time in preparation. They believe spectacular achievements are the result of
unspectacular preparation.

Second, generators are relationship builders. They know that all
things being equal, prospects buy from the sales rep they know,
trust and like. More importantly, they understand that all things
not being equal, buyers do the same thing — they buy from sales
reps they know, trust and like.

Third, generators work at the right things. They focus on those
few sales activities that make the big difference.

Next, generators always have a sales call objective. They have in
mind a "bottom line result" as they enter every selling situation.

Fifth, generators ask probing questions. They ask the right questions — the questions which arouse interest with prospects.

Sixth, generators talk to the decision makers. They do not want to give their presentation for practice.

Finally, generators manage the buying process. They help along the prospects' decision to buy.

> *Generators take chances. They are risk takers.*
> *Like everyone else, they fear failing, but*
> > *refuse to let fear paralyze them.*
> *Generators never give up.*
> *When life gets rough, they hang in until the going gets*
> > *better.*
> *Generators are flexible.*
> *They realize there is more than one way and are willing to*
> > *try others.*
> *Generators focus on excellence, not perfection.*
> *They make the most of their strengths, while respecting*
> > *their weaknesses.*
> *Generators fall, but they get up.*
> *Generators don't blame fate for their failures nor luck for*
> > *their successes.*
> *Generators accept the responsibility for their performance.*
> *Generators are positive thinkers who see possibilities in all*
> > *things.*
> *From the ordinary, they make the extraordinary.*
> *Generators stay on the path they have chosen even when*
> > *it's difficult and others can't see where they are*
> > *going.*
> *Generators are patient and persistent.*
> *They know a goal is only as worthy as the effort required to*
> > *achieve it.*

Nancye Sims

It's easy to see why generators are always the best rewarded in all sales organizations.

> *To each is given a bag of tools,*
> *A shapeless mass,*
> *A book of rules;*
> *Then each must build,*
> *'Ere life is flown,*
> *A stumbling block*
> *Or a stepping stone.*

R. L. Sharpe
American Poet

Positioning Precept
Be A Generator

Make The Telephone Pay

You can't serve the customer and collect a commission until you make a sale. You can't make the sale until you've written up the order. You can't write the order until you get an interview. And, you can't have an interview until you get in!

-Corwin Riley

Elmer Wheeler was a master salesman in his day — and a most effective sales trainer. Wheeler became well known for one statement — *"Sell the sizzle, not the steak!"*

Wheeler made another statement having to do with setting appointments. He said, *"Your first 10 words in selling are more important than your next 10,000."* That's an overstatement for sure. But Elmer Wheeler was attempting to drive home the fact that your early words should be well chosen and well delivered.

Elmer Wheeler was training in a time when most sales calls were being made face-to-face. In most selling positions, the telephone call has replaced the personal visit in making the initial contact with prospects. *The telephone is the one business tool that helps budget time, qualify prospects and enhance your professional image.*

Here are some early words which will serve you well. "Pete?" (response) "This is Jack Smith calling. Is this a convenient time for you to talk?"

Pete will either say, "Yes," "No," or "What's this about?" When Pete says, "Yes," you have permission to talk. If Pete says, "What's this about?," you've been given permission to talk. If he says, "No," you then give Pete a choice of times when you will call back.

When you gain permission to talk, you then proceed with a series of power statements about the benefits of your product or service.

Keep in mind that what a prospect says during the early minutes of your initial contact is seldom an accurate measure of his or her rating as a prospect. Learn to cope with early resistance by following this two-step strategy.

"That's all right, Pete. I can understand why you would say that and I'll take that into consideration when we get together."

If the same objection persists, move ahead by saying — "May I ask, why do you feel that way?" Draw out your prospect with a question.

There are four basic strategies on which your telephone success depends —

- *Having a reason for calling.* Have something to discuss that motivates the person at the other end to want to listen.
- *Being prepared to respond.* Be mentally and physically "ready to strike."
- *Following a prepared script.* Know what you are going to say and how you are going to say it. Your early words are critical to your success.
- *Being brief and conveying a certain sense of urgency.* This you do by speaking a bit faster and louder than normal.

Developing competence and confidence in using the telephone can boost your sales performance dramatically. Here are 12 proven ways to develop your telephone effectiveness. You'll find it helpful to review these often.

1) ***Maintain a positive attitude*** about using the telephone. Know the "dollar value" of each telephone call you make. Stay sold on the law of averages.

2) ***Choose a private place to make your calls*** in order to establish a momentum and to avoid interruptions.

3) ***Organize your calls.*** Have names, numbers and information organized in advance. You'll accomplish more in less time when you do. Your prospects and customers will be impressed by this organization.

4) ***Seek some common ground*** with the person at the other end of the line. Do you have mutual acquaintances? Do you know about his or her company, neighborhood, community involvement, etc.?

5) ***Build and use a script.*** Know exactly what you are going to say and, again, how you are going to say it.

6) ***Introduce yourself, your company and state the purpose of your call immediately.*** Make certain there is no apology or hesitancy in what you say or how you say it.

7) ***Verify the name of the prospect to whom you are speaking.*** Make certain of its pronunciation.

8) ***Speak as if you were with the prospect and looking directly at him or her.*** This helps to establish better rapport. Courtesy, sincerity and clarity of speech will contribute to your success. Use "Thank you," "May I ask," and other expressions that demonstrate good manners. Keep a smile in your voice.

9) ***Be assertive.*** Assertiveness shows itself in your voice quality. When you speak on the telephone, your voice is you and your business. The impression it makes has a big influence on a prospect's decision as to whether or not to give you an appointment. Be and stay enthusiastic — it will come through in your voice.

10)   ***Avoid an argument.*** No matter what the response, stay poised and point toward the setting of an appointment. Use questions that invite "yes" answers. Don't push too hard for an appointment. Never accept an appointment that sounds tentative. Make sure prospects understand your time is valuable.

11)   ***Dial until your allotted time is up.*** If you plan to telephone for two hours, then discipline yourself to dial for two hours.

12)   ***Thank your prospect.*** Always let the prospect hang up first.

The telephone has these advantages:

- The number of calls can be increased.
- Cost per call is reduced.
- Effectiveness may be improved. It is often possible to gain the ear of a busy prospect when you couldn't gain a face-to-face interview.
- Brevity is encouraged. It gains concentration on both ends of the wire.
- You can work rapidly over the telephone and concentrate your personal calls on large buyers, or those who require a visit.
- Opportunity is provided for you to obtain an immediate decision.

This is why you want to perfect your telephone skills and make it pay everyday.

Remember, the first rule of selling is, *"Get in."* If you don't get in, it doesn't matter how good your presentation, how good your product, or how superior the service you offer.

Positioning Precept
Make The Telephone Pay

Understand Buyer's Motives

*If we truly dedicate ourselves to instill that thrill of merchandising
— the thrill of buying and selling something at a profit —
into our salespeople, nothing can ever stop us.
This means that you have the merchandise the
customer wants, when the customer wants it,
and you make it easy for them to buy it.*

-Sam Walton

In its professional sense, the term "sales reps" designates those whose vocation is that of distribution — the direct work of marketing products and services. In its specific sense, to "sell" is to induce the consumer to buy. *The modern-day sales rep who successfully sells induces conscious and willing agreement, resulting in a sale of mutual benefit to both the buyer and seller.*

Most every consumer study suggests people buy your products and services today, not nearly as much because they understand them, but because they sense and believe that you, the sales rep, understand them. In building your sales presentation, you'll want to keep in mind the buying motives. *Everyone who buys does so for one or more of four primary motives. These are protection of life, pleasure in life, pride of ownership, and profit.* Analyze any sale you've ever made. You'll see that consumers' willingness to buy, the actual decision to part with their money, was based upon one or more of these motives.

The prospect's mind is brought into agreement with your mind and the sale is made through the art of persuasion. Persuasion has three functions: 1) a full and complete explanation of the product that causes the prospect to know and to understand; 2) the proper stimulation of the emotional feelings that cause the prospect to believe and to desire; 3) the assisting action that causes the prospect to buy.

Dale Carnegie described persuasion in selling best when he said: *"If you would win a man to your cause, first convince him that you are his true friend. Next, probe to discover what he wants to accomplish. Then, instruct him concerning the merits of your proposition."*

Selling points, proper responses to questions and objections, ready words for turning interruptions into an advantage and closing points must all be presented with appropriate words. You'll, of course, recognize and know which of the buying motives should be given the most emphasis in your presentation. Whatever the motive impelling your prospect to part with his or her money — pleasure, protection, profit, or pride — to this and its related motives you make your appeal.

It can't be repeated too often — *you must remember today's customers are much more sophisticated and much better informed.* Consumers today have learned most of the gimmicks and "high pressure tricks" by which salespeople have attempted to manipulate them. They are much more sensitive to the phony, the insincere, and anything resembling manipulation. *The lesson here: attract favorable attention, inspire confidence, reinforce appreciation of value, allow the prospect to feel and show interest, intensify the desire to own.* Finally, secure satisfaction. The perfect job of salesmanship consists of transferring your conviction to the consumer.

This kind of persuasion is salesmanship and "buymanship" personified.

Positioning Precept
Understand Buyer's Motives

Guide The Buyer's Behavior

What the mind attends to, it considers;
what it does not attend to, it dismisses.
What the mind attends to continually,
it believes. And what the mind
believes, it eventually achieves.

-Napoleon Hill

The psychologist, Pavlov, made a great scientific contribution when he discovered the theory of the "conditioned reflex." Pavlov experimented extensively with dogs, feeding them and simultaneously ringing a bell. The dog learned to associate the sight, taste and the smell of food with the sound of the bell. After a few days, the association between the ringing bell and the eating experience was deeply entrenched in its mind. At this point in his experiment, Pavlov would ring the bell at feeding time but purposely not produce any food. Pavlov now noticed amazing behavior. Even though he didn't provide the dog with food, the dog's entire digestive system responded in the same manner as it did when food was there to satisfy his appetite. He salivated and digestive juices in his stomach were secreted.

The human brain and nervous system are far more advanced and complicated than that of any of Pavlov's dogs. Consumer buying behavior is infinitely more complex. However, extensive research has indicated that customers, too, can be conditioned to react and behave in certain predictable patterns.

There are four steps to guiding the buyer's behavior. *First, give approval — every human being seeks and desires the approval of others. Let them know you recognize them and sincerely desire to understand them as individuals, different from all others.* Search for ways to approve the things your prospects want to accomplish.

Consumers want approval from you more than any other single thing.

Secondly, use the question technique — your prospect must think and pay attention in order to answer questions. By getting your prospects involved in the interview, you make certain they are listening to what you're saying. Listen to your prospects with interest and undivided attention. *Let them feel you want to hear what they have to say.* After they have had a chance to respond, feed it back by summarizing what has been said. In this way, all parties agree on the problem and you're in the perfect position to produce the solution.

Next, use decision — direction statements — "You want to be sure of making the right choice, don't you?" "You understand the wisdom of making this decision today." Or, "Let's consider one additional item that will be important to you." Never lose sight of the fact that *every time your prospect says "Yes" to a minor decision, it makes it easier for them to say "Yes" to the ultimate major decision — the purchase of your products or services.*

The final step is to always serve your customers well. Remember, *your rewards in selling will always be in exact proportion to your service. The better service, the better your rewards.* Always see that you do a little more than is expected. *The successful sales rep is one who sells goods that don't come back, to satisfied customers who do.*

Successful sales reps also embrace the philosophy developed by Henry Drummond when he wrote these words:

> *"I shall pass through this world but once.*
> *Any good, therefore, that I can do,*
> *Or any kindness that I can show,*
> *Let me do it now!*
> *Let me NOT defer or neglect it,*
> *For I shall not pass this way again."*

Success in selling comes to those who learn to guide the consumer's behavior in an effective, low-pressure manner. Guiding the consumer's behavior is a challenging, yet interesting job. Successful salespeople have been doing it for a long time.

Positioning Precept
Guide The Buyer's Behavior

Manage Sales Resistance

Realize resistance doesn't mean denial or refusal.
In selling, its definition means: "Give me a reason to buy!"

-Robert Shook

Today's successful sales reps sell consumer satisfaction ahead of product. Because they are consumer oriented, they know their prospects are more interested in their own problems, needs and wants than in their products and services.

Sal Marino, publisher of the *Steel* magazine, provided the best strategy for managing sales resistance when he said this: *"In the next 24 hours, the buyer's heart will beat 103,689 times, his blood will travel 168,000 miles, his lungs will inhale and exhale 23,240 times, he'll eat over three pounds of food, he'll exercise only seven million of his nine billion brain cells, he'll speak 4,800 words, and not a single one about your product or service - unless you figure out a way to involve him emotionally with your sales proposition. Since two-thirds of his conversation for the day will be about himself and his problems, your only way to get your share of those words is to make yourself part of his world."* That last sentence is something that should be emblazoned on the wall in words of fire in order for you to manage sales resistance successfully.

The sales interview is never to be considered as a contest between you and the consumer. If it is, you'll unwillingly act like a contestant and cast your prospect in the role of an opponent. Always conceive of the sales interview as purely a matter of getting emotionally involved, as Mr. Marino suggests, and catering to what your prospect needs and wants.

Successful selling requires that you organize your sales presentation in a manner which will overcome most sales resistance and objections before they come up. When your prospect says, "I want to think it over" or "I want to compare," there's a strong chance he or she doesn't realize how the benefits to be derived from your product will provide more value than it costs. Resistance is the one sure way your prospects have of telling you that you have missed the mark. *They feel you want more from them than you are giving to them in the way of "owner benefits."*

Continue to be consumer oriented rather than product oriented. It will pay you big dividends. It will help you always understand that, although a lot of people should have what you are selling, they will never buy it until you "make yourself a part of their world" — help them want what you have to sell.

That's managing sales resistance!

Positioning Precept
Manage Sales Resistance

Close Sales Confidently

*A great salesperson is one who can close the sale
and get the order — and the reorder — from a prospect
who is already doing business with someone else.*

-Harvey B. Mackay

It's trite to say, "Nothing happens until the sale is closed." But it's true. Closing sales is the main objective. This is the high pay-off.

Students of selling have discovered the reason why buyers often act so unnatural at the buying moment. This reason is one of the big things for you to learn if you are to improve "your batting average" in closing sales.

Psychologists have proven now beyond any doubt that at the moment of buying, buyers are not normal in their behaviors. They really become abnormal. Dr. Donald Laird, at Colgate University, tells us that the reactions of buyers are more like those of a crowd than those of an individual. Crowds do not reason. Crowds are easily influenced if the individual providing the leadership knows the right principles to employ.

What it boils down to is this: If you want to close more sales, you must understand the situation. *At the moment of closing, you are dealing with a nervous, emotional, abnormal "mind of the crowd."* A buying complex comes over your prospects, and changes them entirely. This is a situation you must face and learn to handle if you are to move into the big league in selling.

Sales reps who go to the top and stay there understand how these five basic closing principles help them deal with the buyer complex — and close more and better sales.

Study each of these important principles carefully.

1) **Speak as one who has authority.** You'll develop this skill only by becoming over-rehearsed. Research the content of your presentation. Practice your lines. See yourself in action in front of a mirror. Record your words and examine your delivery. *Instead of asking for the order, instruct your prospects, with conviction, on what they should do. You're the knowledgeable professional — the authority.* When you act like it, more prospects will act on your recommendations.

2) **Project positive expectations.** Your verbal and non-verbal communication should send a clear message that says, "I'm expecting to get the order today." Expect success.

3) **Be easy to buy from.** Speak the prospect's language, not industry jargon. Sell at the buyer's pace. Some will want to move quickly and buy impulsively. Others will be comfortable only when moving slowly and buying cautiously. You must stay "in-step" with buyers if you're to close sales effectively.

4) **Be difficult to say "No" to.** Display evidence of your preparation. Develop "mini- commitments" as you move along. Gain understanding. Be orderly when using support materials. Project professionalism. These are the things which obligate prospects. These are the things which motivate them to take action. *Remember, prospects don't care how much you know, until they know how much you care.*

5) **Make the strategic move.** This happens the instant you begin to write on the order blank. *You have now started in motion something your prospect must stop. Otherwise, he or she has given you an implied consent to continue and complete the transaction.*

Here's the most helpful philosophy we've ever come across on closing. It was written by Charles Roth. Reflect on it often. It's sure to strengthen your closing efforts.

> *"If an individual can't go out and close sales that do*
> *not close themselves; can't make up the customers'*
> *minds for them; can't direct their thoughts into proper*
> *channels, overcome their fears and their tendencies to*
> *procrastinate, this individual isn't a sales rep at all. He*
> *or she is merely a conversationalist!"*

The most important factor in closing sales is not the customer. It's not the product. It's not the price. It's not the terms. It's not the weather or business conditions. *It's you — the individual behind the sale — the closer who is thinking right and who has mastered these five closing principles.*

Positioning Precept
Close Sales Confidently

Develop Endorsements

*No advertising is as trusted as the spontaneous
testimony of delighted customers.*

-Betsy Sanders

Betsy Sanders, former Vice President of Nordstrom's, has written a wonderful book, *Fabled Service.* In this book, Betsy shares her secrets for creating legendary customer service. We'd like for you to read again the quote taken from *Fabled Service* at the top of this page. If you believe in her philosophy, as we do, you'll have sufficient motivation for going all out to achieve customer satisfaction everytime. Moreover, you'll be positioned to ask a very key question after every sale — *"Who is more approachable now as a result of my having made this sale?"*

There is a proven procedure which will serve you well throughout your selling career. It's this — *Develop endorsements, not referrals.*

How do you do this? First, you understand a basic fact about human nature. *All of us like approval of our decisions.* In other words, your new customers would like nothing more than to have contacts of theirs make purchases from you. *This action is supportive of their decisions to buy.*

Secondly, you need a simple strategy, a sales script you can use confidently. We've used this one for years —

> Tom, I need to ask you to help me. We study our business closely. Recently, we made an interesting discovery. Nearly 75 percent of our new customer base comes from satisfied customers like you.

139

> I plan to call on David Smith. I know David is a close friend and contact of yours.
>
> Let me ask you a question, Tom. Do you like getting cold calls from salespeople you do not know?
>
> Of course not, and neither do I. In fact, there's only one thing I know of I dislike more than receiving a cold call — and that's making one!
>
> You can help me take "the cold" out of my call to David Smith by ...

Now, depending upon circumstances, you may ask Tom to write a short note, make a call or even set up a meeting for you with David.

Don't miss the power of this strategy. It works! Customers, especially satisfied customers, love to help you. Give them that opportunity, and watch your sales jump!

Positioning Precept
Develop Endorsements

Express Appreciation

The habit of expressing thanks should carry over into all areas of our lives, and has particular importance to business. Be alert for chances to express your gratitude to those who have helped or extended a courtesy or kindness. It will set you apart.

-Bob Briner

Your customers have one thing in common — *each one is hungry for sincere appreciation.* Most feel that others do not recognize or appreciate their true worth. Praise and appreciation can work wonders in building long lasting, viable relationships.

Here's an interesting illustration:

> In the Fall of 1860, the steamship "Lady Elgin" set out with a total of 393 passengers and crew members, to make the trip from Chicago to Milwaukee. Just off the shore of Evanston, she was rammed by a lumber schooner and sank. As a result, 279 of the passengers and crew members died. Of those who were saved, 17 of them were saved by Edward W. Spence, a student at Northwestern University. He made 16 trips in all from the shore to the sinking ship and back again, saving the 17 lives.

> Because of physical exertion and the coldness of the water, Spence was in shock at the end of the 16th trip. It was reported that as they carried him to the hospital, he kept asking the question *"Did I do my best?"*

> As a result of the incident, Edward Spence spent the remainder of his life as an invalid in a wheelchair.

Fifty years later, Northwestern granted him a Bachelor of Arts degree. Not because he ever finished the class work - he didn't. He was awarded the degree because they decided he deserved it. It was at that time that the plaque commemorating his heroism was placed on the wall of the old Coast Guard Station at the southeast corner of the campus. It hangs there yet today.

When he was 80 years old, Edward Spence was interviewed by Chicago newspaper reporters. They asked him *"What is your most vivid memory of that tragic Fall day when the "Lady Elgin" went down off the coast of Evanston?"* Mr. Spence's answer was, *"The fact that not one of the 17 people whose lives I saved ever came back to say thank you. Not one."*

People want recognition as individuals more than any other single thing. Even those who never perform a heroic act.

Consider how you feel when someone shows you sincere appreciation — or they neglect to do so. Sincere appreciation gives you a lift. You develop a feeling of kinship and liking for the person who takes the time to appreciate you. You want to create these same feelings in your customers. You might ask, "Why don't more people use this technique?" This is a question that has no logical answer. Properly used, praise and appreciation are strong factors in building and maintaining relationships.

The question you want to ask again and again is, *"What can I do to favorably stand out in my customer's mind so that he or she comes back and refers others?"* We've always liked what Harvey Mackay said: *"In building lasting relationships, little things don't mean alot — they mean everything."*

To become an effective relationship builder, start looking for ways in which you can express appreciation. You have, of course, some natural times when you should always show your appreciation:

- **Express appreciation for each order received.** Appreciation for new orders is always an automatic. Fax or mail a "thank you" note within 24 hours.

- **Express appreciation to those who assist you.** It's good to give appreciation to those who assist you in any way to reach and sell your new customer. These might include receptionists, assistants, secretaries, etc. They can be most helpful to you in building a relationship.

- **Always express appreciation for an interview.** You should always give appreciation to the prospect who gives you an interview, even if he or she does not buy. This is one of the best ways to make an impression and to keep the prospect's mind open to your proposition at a future date. When the need or opportunity arises to consider a change, he or she will have good reason to remember you.

- **Show appreciation through your manners and actions.** Your manners and actions reveal your appreciation. Let the buyer know where you can be reached whenever you are needed. This tells your customer you appreciate his or her business and want to keep it. Returning telephone calls promptly shows your appreciation, as does being an attentive listener.

- **Look for opportunities.** Look for opportunities to recognize any special occasions or achievements. It shows your interest. Scout trade papers, local papers and the like for news of promotions or advancements.

- **Give thanks for referrals.** Always express appreciation to those customers who refer business to you. By all means, report back to them on your results.

- **Send prospects to your customers.** If your customers are also in business, send them prospects or supply them with leads. This is an effective way to develop an ongoing relationship. It is just natural for a person to respond favorably to you when you show your appreciation and helpfulness.

The basic principle to follow is this one: *Never forget a customer and never let a customer forget you.*

Positioning Precept
Express Appreciation

Serve What You Sell

*Standards of absolutely first-class, pristine performers don't
spontaneously emerge. Standards of excellence are
cultivated by first-class salespeople committed
to the notion that second-best simply won't do.*

-Dr. Michael H. Mescon

Companies rarely have a product design or price advantage for
very long. Their competitive edge, their only major advantage, lies
in the professional manner in which their salespeople deliver
distinctive service. Your image in business circles and your
community has a *direct bearing* on your sales performance.

*After the sale is buttoned up and the order signed is the time to
remember that customers who purchased the products and paid for
them did so because they had confidence in the sales rep and the
service that sales rep would provide.* Whether or not that confidence will be maintained and even enhanced depends largely upon
the manner in which the sale after the sale is handled.

Professionalism in selling requires prompt, personal follow-
through. As Dr. Mike Mescon, Dean of the Business School at
Georgia State, says, *"Good or bad, right or wrong, clients are
most likely to recall the last - not the first - experience. They
remember the end of the story, not the beginning. Clients want
consistent service from start to finish."* As a professional, you
want to deliver consistent service and achieve customer satisfaction.

Strive to make customer satisfaction your "stock-in-trade." How do
you do this? *Quite* simply: *Make certain your prospects get more
in the way of service from you than they expect. Make certain they
get more than they pay for. And make certain they get more in the*

145

way of service and information from you than they can possibly get from your competitors.

We believe that as a professional salesperson, you will be judged as much by the customers you keep as by the sales you make. What are some of the things you can do to make your sales stay closed by means of good post-selling techniques?

- **First, you can assure your new client that he or she has made an intelligent decision.** An effective way to do this is to write a congratulatory letter. This adds a distinctive touch. It displays professionalism. Many of your competitors will not be as well organized or take the time to write.

- **Second, look for communications opportunities.** There are many reasons you can find to send business, prospects, or information to prospects and clients. Ask yourself this question regularly — *"What can I do to help my customer's business?"*

- **Next, after your product or idea has been installed, make follow-up, courtesy calls regularly.** This eyeball-to-eyeball exposure with the new customer permits you to accomplish several important objectives. It permits you to resell the need for the product and, naturally, in talking to satisfied customers, you can get them thinking about future additional purchases.

- **Finally, frequent in-person contacts with new customers make it possible for you to get approvals and endorsements.** Your best prospects will be developed in this manner. Satisfied customers will help recommend you, your products and services. Every time you make a sale, you should ask yourself this question, "Who can I approach and sell a bit easier now because I made this sale?" Once you've sold a customer, make sure he or she is satisfied with your product and you. Stay with customers until the goods are used up or worn out. Your product may be of such long life that you'll never sell them again, but they will sell you and your product to their friends and contacts.

Remember, it takes less effort to keep an existing customer satisfied than to get a new prospect interested. Your customers will be presented claims and counter-claims from people who offer similar products at about the same price. The competitive edge you want to develop comes from the attitude you project of serving as you sell. You do this in two ways.

- **First, you do whatever it takes to establish a record of consistent reliability.** Earning the reputation of being a 100 percent reliable sales rep whose every word and promise can be depended upon takes application, effort and attention to detail.

- **Second, you stay determined to be the best-informed sales rep who calls on your customers.** This requires a commitment to excellence and a regular program of study.

Once you have established the image of being a reliable, well-informed salesperson, you are in an enviable position.

Again, the basic principle is: *Never forget a customer. Never let a customer forget you.*

Positioning Precept
Serve What You Sell

Precept Supporting Philosophies

The will to succeed is important, but what's more important is the will to prepare.
>   — Bobby Knight

Enthusiasm for your product and life is the most precious ingredient in any recipe for greatness in selling. And the finest feature of this ingredient is that it is available to everyone.
>   — Samuel Goldwyn

Selling success is turning knowledge into positive action.
>   — Dorothy Leeds

Nothing is often a good thing to do, and almost always a clever thing to say.
>   — Will Durant

Underpromise, overdeliver. Customers expect you to keep your word. Exceed it.
>   — Carl Sewell

The best ways to keep customers coming back are: be believable, credible, attractive, responsive and empathic. Reliable care keeps customers coming back.
>   — Michael LeBoeuf, Ph.D.

The sales rep who cannot persuade, who cannot direct customer's thoughts into proper channels, overcome their resistance and tendency to procrastinate, isn't a sales rep at all. He or she is merely a conversationalist.
>   — Charles Roth

Off The Professionals' Bookshelf

Barnett, Dr. David K. *Earning What You're Worth.* Behavioral Sciences Research Press, Inc.

Carnegie, Dale. *How To Win Friends And Influence People.* Simon & Schuster, 1981.

Dudley, George W. and Shannon Goodwon. *The Psychology of Call Reluctance.* Behavioral Science research, 1986.

Hopkins, Tom. *How To Master The Art of Selling.* Tom Hopkins, Inc., Warner, 1982.

Malloy, John T. *Dress For Success.* Warner Books, 1976.

Mandino, Og. *The Greatest Salesman In The World.* Bantam Books, 1987.

McCormick, Mark H. *The 100% Solution.* Villard Books.

Nelson, Oliver *Ziglar on Selling,* 1991

Roth, Charles. *Secrets Of Closing.* Prentice-Hall, 1993.

Sewell, Carl. *Customers For Life.* Pocket Books, 1990.

Stanley, Thomas J. *Selling To The Affluent.* Business One Irwin.

Todd, John. *Ceiling Unlimited.* Field, 1965.

Ziglar, Zig. *Ziglar On Selling.* Oliver Nelson, 1991

Competency Builders

There is one straight road to success in selling. It's "paved"
with knowledge. Competency never lacks opportunity.
It will not remain undiscovered because it's respected
by too many people anxious to benefit from it.

Be A Student Of Selling

In a world of change, you are never completely educated.
You must keep educating yourself to cope with change.
The more you learn about your job, the
less fear there is. Fear is born out of ignorance.
When you empty your purse into your head, no
one can take it away from you.

-James A. Lovell

We recommend you carry Frank Bettger's wonderful book, *How I Raised Myself From Failure To Success In Selling*, in your briefcase. Review it each week, at least during the early years of your sales career. This will encourage you to visit it whenever you have some unplanned waiting time.

These insights, gained from the Bettger book, will prove to be invaluable to you.

1)   **Take the time to think and do things in the order of their importance**. One of the greatest satisfactions in life comes from getting things done and knowing you've done them to the best of your ability.

2)   **Sell yourself on you first.** This is the most important sale you'll make.

3)   **The single most important secret of successful selling is to find out what your prospects want and then help them discover the best way to get it.** This is a selling strategy to live by.

4) **There is only one way to get people motivated to do anything and that's to make the other person want to do it.** There's just no other way. Make it their idea.

5) **Develop confidence builders.** Learn the benefits of planning priorities. Be over-rehearsed. These are confidence builders. Use confidence building statements with prospects! "If you were my own brother (or sister), I'd say to you what I'm going to say to you now." "That sounds right." "The really significant thing is ..." "So your question is ..."

6) **Cultivate the art of asking questions.** Using questions, rather than positive statements, can be the most effective means for winning people to your way of thinking. Inquire rather than attack. There are six things you gain by the question method. It helps avoid arguments. It helps avoid talking too much and enables you to help prospects recognize what they want. It helps crystallize the prospects' thinking, making the idea their idea. It helps you find the most vulnerable point with which to close the sale (the key issue); it gives your prospects the feeling of importance. When you respect your prospects' opinions, they are more likely to respect yours.

7) **The prospect generally has two reasons for doing any thing.** One that sounds good and the real one.

8) **Build a collection of power statements.** "I want to make certain I understand how you feel." "In addition to that, isn't there something else in the back of your mind?," "I need to ask you ...," "May I ask, do you feel ..."

9) **Listen to learn.** The forgotten art in selling is that of listening. Ask your prospect, "How did you happen to get started in this business?" This will force you to listen.

10)   **Deserve confidence.** Know your business, and keep on knowing your business.

11)   **Bring on your witnesses.** This builds credibility. If someone your prospect respects has made the decision to buy from you, then they feel it must be good.

12)   **Be brief.** You can't know too much, but you can talk too much.

13)   **Write out your sales talk, word-for-word.** Give it until you love its sound.

14)   **Never forget a customer.** Never let a customer forget you.

15)   **The best time to follow-up on a lead is in the next six minutes.**

16)   **A good summation sets up the best foundation for a successful climax in selling.**

17)   **Let the prospect help you make the sale.** After concluding the presentation, ask the prospect, "How do you like it?" and "Does this do the things you want done?"

18)   **Keep accurate records of calls and interviews.** There is strong motivation in knowing the dollar value of each telephone call, each interview, each presentation and each referral.

19)   **Attend as many sales clinics as you possibly can.** If you get only one idea, the time and money you invest will be the best investment you'll ever make.

20)   **Stick with it.** Success in selling is measured by the number of successful acts you produce, not by the number you experience along the way. Failures mean nothing if success eventually comes.

There you have the "Best of Bettger." Review his sales ideas often. They will sharpen your selling skills and build your confidence in dealing with prospects.

Positioning Precept
Be A Student Of Selling

Prepare Well

*I expect to spend the rest of my life in the future, so
I want to be reasonably sure of what kind of future
it's going to be. That is my reason for planning.*

-Charles F. Kettering

On finishing a concert, the great violinist, Fritz Kreisler was approached by an elderly lady who said, "Mr. Kreisler, I would give my life to be able to play a violin like that." *"Madam,"* said Fritz Kreisler, *"I did."*

Spectacular performances are always preceded by unspectacular preparation.

It's the same in the sales world. Many people look at the stars in selling and say, "I wish I could perform like they do; I wish I had their knowledge, their contacts." When salespeople say that, they don't really mean it. *They want the high achievers' skills, and of course, their incomes — but as for the years of unspectacular preparation — that is another matter.*

We must be prepared. We must be well versed on our subject. We must know our product, backward and forward. We must know our prospects' businesses and know how we can best serve them. We have to put in hours and hours of unspectacular preparation so that we can come up with a spectacular performance at the time of the sales interview.

Ron Price, a good friend of ours and a great sales executive, has said, *"Salespeople achieve new peaks in performance when they have the know-how, the skill, the enthusiasm and the will to achieve."* We agree with Ron that personal success and new peaks in performance will always be achieved by those who are willing to pay the price.

Many times that price comes in the form of hard work, study, and the everyday drudgery of doing the things that the unsuccessful refuse to do. This is that unspectacular preparation which always precedes spectacular sales results.

In your preparation for building a firm foundation for success in selling, here are a few stones to include:

> *The value of confidence*
> *The worth of honesty*
> *The privilege of working*
> *The discipline of struggle*
> *The magnetism of character*
> *The radiance of health*
> *The effectiveness of simplicity*
> *The winsomeness of courtesy*
> *The satisfaction of serving*
> *The power of suggestion*
> *The buoyancy of enthusiasm*
> *The advantage of initiative*
> *The virtue of patience*
> *The rewards of cooperation*
> *The fruitfulness of perseverance*
> *The joy of winning*
> *The wisdom of preparation.*
>
> Rollo C. Hester

Michelangelo said, *"Trifles make perfection, and perfection is no trifle."*

Prepare well. Be a spectacular performer!

Positioning Precept
Prepare Well

Develop A Mentor

My Dad taught me when I was little,
young doesn't learn from young.
Young learns from old. Period!

-Steve Elkington

We've been telling our sales audiences for years to include in their personal libraries every book authored by Og Mandino. He is arguably the finest self-help author our country has ever produced.

Og Mandino is an equally gifted speaker. A few years back, we heard him tell a story to a Dallas audience, a story that we have never forgotten. His story, which follows, drives home the theme, *Develop A Mentor.*

> *We all need help to achieve, to grow, to recover from setbacks. Back in the 15th Century, in a little village right outside of Nuremberg, Germany, lived a family with fifteen children. Daddy worked three jobs — just to keep food on the table for this tribe. Two of the boys had an ambition, a dream. It was the same dream. They both wanted to go to the Art Academy in Nuremberg. But they knew full well that there was no way their daddy would ever be able to afford to send either one of them.*
>
> *So these two brothers, with similar talents and interests, worked up a pact. They would toss a coin. The winner would go to the academy. The loser would go down into the*

mines, and with his pay, would support the winner's studies. Four years later, when the first one was graduated, he would go into the mines or use the income from his commissioned artwork to support his brother, who would attend the academy and obtain his art degree, too.

One morning they tossed the coin. Albrecht Durer won. Albert Durer lost. Albrecht went off to the academy, and Albert went down into the mines.

Albrecht was an immediate sensation at the academy. He was better than any of his professors. In his paintings, in his line drawings, in his engravings, in his woodcuts - he was just a natural. By his third year in school, Albrecht was earning enough in commissions to support himself. And when he graduated, the family held a large party out on the lawn. All the children were there. Albrecht, from the head of the table, arose with a glass of wine. He offered a toast to his beloved brother, for all that Albert had done for him. And he finished the toast by saying, " ... and now, Albert — now it's your turn. You can go to the academy, and I will take care of you."

All eyes turned to the other end of the table. Albert was staring down at his hands and shaking his head saying, "No, no, no."

Finally Albert rose, tears streaming down his cheeks. He looked down at Albrecht and said,

*"Albrecht, dear brother, it's too late for me.
Look what four years in the mines have done
to my hands! I've broken every finger at least
once. I have arthritis in my left hand so bad
that I can't even hold a piece of bread. I
can't even lift my hands together so that I
could return your toast properly. No,
brother, I love you, but it is too late, much too
late for me."*

*Four hundred years have passed. Albrecht
Durer's artwork hangs in every great museum
in the world. And yet, most know him for just
one of his creations. Because one day,
Albrecht Durer honored his beloved brother
by painting his hands.*

*Some of you have it hanging in your home.
Or, maybe, you wear it around your neck as a
charm. Maybe you have it in your office as
bookends. But I know all of you know it.
Because today we call it "The Praying
Hands."*

When you look at that marvelous piece of work — study it carefully. Let it remind you of the common thread that runs through the life of every true success story in selling. *No sales rep - no matter how great — achieves outstanding success alone.*

Like all the rest, you need help to learn, to grow and to develop your skills. You'll be surprised how close that help is, if you attract, nurture and develop a mentor.

The first mentor was a woman, Athena, the Greek goddess of wisdom. She took the form of a male tutor named Mentor in order to coach Telemachus, the son of Homer's hero Odysseus.

Ever since, mentors have been important to professionals who are searching for "the better way."

Here are a dozen things a mentor will contribute to your success in selling:

- *Expects the best of you.*
- *Helps you short-cut time.*
- *Always available.*
- *Source of encouragement.*
- *Serves as "sounding board."*
- *Source of knowledge and expertise.*
- *Provides network of contacts.*
- *Holds you to high standards of performance.*
- *Exhibits concern about your professional growth.*
- *Interested in your personal development.*
- *Promotes you to others.*
- *Serves as a valuable role model.*

Remember, when selecting a mentor, search for the individual traveling "the same road" you're traveling — and one who is out in front.

Positioning Precept
Develop A Mentor

Watch Your Self-Talk

No person is what he thinks he is,
but what he thinks — he is.

-Robert Anthony

Self-talk shapes your selling life. Have you seen the breathtaking pillars in Mammoth Cave in Kentucky? Those enormous "icicles of stone" have taken centuries to form. A single drop of water finds its way through the roof of the cavern to deposit its tiny sediment on the floor of the cave. Another drop follows, and still another, until a marble-like finger begins to grow upward. The result is a tremendously solid pillar.

Self-talk shapes your life in much the same way. What you are is the result of the many accumulated statements you have made and continue to make with your self-talk.

What have you told yourself today? What conversation has gone on in your head? What have you hidden in your heart? Has it been positive statements of self-affirmation? That's the kind of self-talk required to be and stay at your best.

Take charge of your thoughts. They are yours to control. Monitor what you are telling yourself about your situation and about your potential in selling.

When you have identified a self-statement, the first question to ask is this: "Is it true?" Sometimes you'll discover you are telling yourself things that are not true.

Charlie "Tremendous" Jones describes himself in the days when he was a young trainee life insurance agent. Charlie says he could look at a front door and with absolute certainty tell himself, "Those folks are not prospects. They would not buy anything from me!" You know — and he knows — that he was telling himself something that might not have been true.

Many times we tell ourselves things that are not necessarily true. "I'm not experienced enough. I'm not knowledgeable enough. I need to be better connected with the prospect. I'm not effective in that market." Ask yourself: "Is this really true?" Many times these statements are not true. But if your self-talk includes those statements, you begin to perform as if they were true.

Sometimes we make self-statements that are only partially true. The problem is you respond as if the statement were entirely true.

Suppose you check your self-talk and discover you are telling yourself you have trouble closing sales. Remember, the first question to ask is: "Is that really true?" Suppose the answer is "Yes, sometimes it is true." The next question is: "O.K. Is it 100 percent true?" "Is it 60 percent true?" Let's say it's true 60 percent of the time. You have trouble closing sales 60 percent of the time. Great! This means it's not true 40 percent of the time. Change your self-talk. You can now confidently say, "40 percent of the time I'm effective closing sales." What a difference! You're now building a mental image of one who can do it right. And the 40 percent will soon become 50 percent and 60 percent. Self-talk makes a difference.

Jack Paar, the original Tonight Show host, said, *"My life is like one long obstacle course with me being the chief obstacle."* Don't let your self-talk be the chief obstacle in your selling life. Self-talk is yours to control. Don't let your self-talk make you second-class. Identify what you are telling yourself. If it's negative, challenge it. Then correct it.

"Dunce" was the word indelibly printed in Victor's mind. That's what others said. That's what he told himself. A dunce does not finish school. So at fifteen, he dropped out. And for the next 17 years, he lived out what his self-talk described — dunce.

At the age of 32, Victor Seribriakoff was transformed. An IQ test resulted in a score of 161 - a genius! But that was not the transformation. He had had a brilliant mind all the time. *The transformation came because he now believed he was a genius.* His self-talk said, "I'm a genius — not a dunce." He acted like a genius. He thought like a genius. He worked like a genius.

Seribriakoff was ultimately elected chairman of the International Mensa Society, a group requiring an IQ of at least 140 for membership. Victor Seribriakoff changed his self-talk. It changed his life.

Shakespeare's Marcus Aurelius said, *"Your life is an expression of all your thoughts."* Check your self-talk. It may be the difference between being a "dunce" and a "genius" in selling for you.

Positioning Precept
Watch Your Self-Talk

Stay Brilliant On The Basics

*Effective selling involves not only the power of persuasion,
the art of negotiation, persistence and timing — it also demands,
as much as any of these, the proper marketability of your product.*

-Mark McCormack

Whether or not the prospect is willing to buy depends largely on his or her internal feelings at the time. *These feelings are strongly influenced by the prospect's perception of what you say and do, how you act and whether or not you are perceived as being trust-worthy.* Since prospects act on the basis of what they perceive, you must form the habit of saying and doing those things which will cause prospective customers to perceive you as being trust-worthy.

Stay brilliant on these basics:

- **Build credibility.** This starts with preparation. You should have already developed enough information to be fully convinced that what you recommend is truly in the prospect's best interest. Demonstrate a sincere interest in the prospect as a person as early as possible. Build the trust level quickly. Use referral influence up front, whenever you can. The fact that other people, respected by the prospect, have found you trust-worthy, creates the impression that you are trustworthy. Convey the impression you expect to be believed and trusted.

- **Be well-mannered.** This may seem to go without saying, but liberal use of phrases like, *"May I ask ..."* or *"If it's all right with you ..." "Let's ..."* tend to win the confidence of prospects. They build your image as a mature, likable person.

- **Simplify your suggestions.** The power of your recommendations will always lie in their simplicity.

- **Speak the prospect's language.** Stay away from industry jargon. Keep your explanations simple as you focus on "owner benefits."

- **Speak as one having authority.** Develop the "lean on me" attitude. Show enthusiasm for your suggestions. Human emotions are highly transferable. Look and speak in terms of success. Prospects like to buy from salespeople they perceive as being successful.

- **Sell at the buyer's pace.** Let prospects interrupt you — but never interrupt your prospects.

- **Avoid the overstatement.** It can imply the prospect is naive. It can result in lack of belief regarding anything else you say.

- **Avoid dogmatic statements.** Skillful salespeople say, *"Many of our customers have found it best to ..."* and *"Others have said ..."* instead of, *"The only sound way to do this, is ..."*

- **Use repetition.** Repetition overcomes communication difficulties. Attempt to make your meaning clear by giving more details, by furnishing examples and by making analogies. Repeated assertion is hard to resist. The initial reaction of the human mind is to reject anything new. This natural, instinctive reaction is a healthy one, because it causes the prospect to think of the pros and cons of the idea and to avoid impulsive decisions he or she might later regret. However, if something is repeated over and over, the prospect's "natural defenses" tend to weaken, because the idea is no longer "new." The tendency is to then admit that "it might be a good idea" and the prospect moves closer to acceptance.

- **Make it the prospect's idea.** Each of us is best convinced by reasons we ourselves discover. Be judged an expert without "flaunting" your knowledge. Avoid even the slightest appearance of feeling superior to the prospect.

- **Summarize strategically.** *"Let's examine again ..."* Cement in the owner benefits. Make certain you have gained understanding.

- **Close with confidence.** Master and perfect your strategy for securing action on your recommendations. Close by assuming. Close by assisting the buyer.

You'll want to review these presentation principles frequently. They go to the heart of the decision-making process the prospect moves through in deciding whether or not to buy what you have to sell.

Positioning Precept
Stay Brilliant On The Basics

Achieve Competency Levels

The books we need to make us as rich, as effective,
as healthy, as powerful, as sophisticated and as
successful as we want to be — have already been written.

-E. James Rohn

Confounded by a defect in a complex system of machines, General Electric's experts called upon retired electrical engineer Charles Steinmetz for assistance.

After walking around and testing various devices, Steinmetz produced a piece of chalk from his pocket and drew an "X" on a specific part of the machine. GE workers disassembled the machine and found that the fault lay exactly where the "X" was located by Steinmetz.

Steinmetz sent General Electric a bill for $10,000. When they protested, Steinmetz mailed an itemized charge:

Making one chalk mark - $1
Knowing where to place it - $9,999

It works pretty much the same in selling. *In selling, there's no substitute for knowing.* This gives meaning to Charley Jones' well-known, classical statement. Charley says it this way, *"Five years from today, you'll be about the same person you are today except for the books you read, the cassettes you view or listen to, and the people from whom you learn."*

There are three levels of competency you want to achieve. *First, is to know. Then, demonstrate you know that you know, by putting into action your knowledge. Finally, become known for what you know.* This is the high payoff. Now your reputation precedes you.

In every line of selling, it's always the competent who are the best paid. *They earn more because they know more.* It's just as simple as that.

They know more about people. They study what makes them "tick." Why prospects buy and how they buy.

Competent salespeople study their product and services. They intend to be the best informed salesperson their customers deal with.

Competent salespeople study their selling procedure. They are conversational with their sales language. The words they use are learned and are delivered as naturally as breathing.

Competent salespeople study personal strengths. They know they are good and they know why they are good.

Competent salespeople study their performance. Each week, at the end of the week, they evaluate their progress toward goals and examine their plan for next week. They are determined to "wake up employed" on Monday morning.

The formula for success is unchanging, and it's easy to follow: *Practice a few simple disciplines every selling day.* One of those disciplines is to deposit in your "competency bank" information and ideas which will make you do better and be better.

Positioning Precept
Achieve Competency Levels

Write Effectively

People judge you by what you say and write.
I don't know a successful person in business
who is not a good letter writer.

-L. A. McQueen

Author Elmore Leonard says, *"the key to writing a best seller is to make sure you leave out the words and sentences the reader skips."* It's the same with letters and memos. T*he best ones get to the point with a minimum word count.*

The chances are you will make contact with at least 10 people by letter each week. You will write to give information, arouse interest and/or show appreciation. The important thing is to keep your name and your company's name in front of a definite number of people each week.

"Simplicity is the formula for successful communication," according to Dr. Rudolf Flesch. Yes, the power of your written messages will lie in their simplicity. These are the rules for writing effectively and achieving simplicity.

- Use "congratulations" and "thank you" at the start.
- Send special notes on special days.
- Put yourself in the reader's place.
- Write about people, things and facts.
- Talk with the reader.

- Use the magic word — you.
- Personalize your message.
- Use contractions.
- Keep your sentences short.
- Keep your paragraphs short.

- Quote what was said in follow-up letters.
- Use testimonials.
- Plan a beginning, middle and end.
- Use pronouns rather than repeating nouns.
- Use verbs rather than nouns.

- Use illustrations, cases and examples.
- Start a new sentence for each new idea.
- Underline, use bold or italics for emphasis.
- Make it easy to respond.
- Make your writing have eye appeal.

- Include a postscript.
- Use enclosures of interest.

Letters and memos are effective ways to communicate. There is power in the written word. The written word has permanency. It can be shared and displayed. It can be typed or handwritten. It sends a message that you care.

Positioning Precept
Write Effectively

Develop The Slight Edge

*Enthusiasm is the prime method of persuasion
without pressure. Enthusiasm is the yeast that
raises the dough. Enthusiasm is the greatest
one-word slogan for living ever devised.*

-Frank Bettger

We made reference to the legendary Frank Bettger earlier in this
section. Here's the story of this remarkable insurance salesman,
and how he got that way. Frank Bettger was a struggling professional baseball player for the New Haven, Connecticut team. At
the time, New Haven was a team in the lowest league in organized
baseball. An amazing thing happened to Frank Bettger at New
Haven. It was a "believe it or not" event. An event never before
or since recorded in the history of professional baseball. Frank
Bettger moved all the way from New Haven, the D-league, the
lowest league at that time, up to the big leagues as a third baseman
for the St. Louis Cardinals. And he did it in less than 60 days.
Now how did he do it? What were the lessons he learned that
made such a big difference in his play?

The first lesson came the day he was fired and sent down to New
Haven. Bill Kahn, his manager at the time told him, *"Frank, you
need to wake yourself up and put some life and some enthusiasm
into your work."* Frank made up his mind to act like a player
electrified and to establish a reputation as the most enthusiastic
baseball player the fans had ever seen. He figured if he established
this kind of reputation, he'd have to live up to it. His greatest thrill
came the morning following his first game. The New Haven
newspaper said, *"This new player Bettger has a barrel of enthusiasm. He has inspired the local ball club. They not only won, they
looked good."* The newspaper started calling him "Pep Bettger."
*He now had a reputation to live up to. But more importantly,
Frank Bettger had learned a great lesson. Feelings follow actions.*

Bettger learned another motivational truth. The second lesson had to do with what we call *The Slight Edge Principle.* It's very important. *This principle has to do with what a slight improvement in one skill can do to one's performance over a period of time.* Bettger's batting average was .238. But batting averages can change. Bettger decided to change his. Each morning he devoted two hours to improving his batting swing. This resulted in only a small improvement. Only one additional hit every 20 times up. But that little difference raised his batting average to over .300. He led the New England League and he was on his way to join the St. Louis Cardinals.

The story continues. After playing with the Cardinals for a few years, an injury to his throwing arm brought Bettger's baseball career to an end. After baseball, Bettger tried several jobs including selling life insurance. He amazed the agency he worked for in Philadelphia. They couldn't believe how anyone could make as many calls and sell no one.

Bettger was on his way to failure again. His highest hope was to get his old job back collecting installments at $18.00 a week. Frank had left a few personal things at the insurance office. So one morning he decided to go back and get them. He expected to be there only a few minutes, but while cleaning out his desk, the President of the company, Mr. Walter Talbot, and all of the agents came into the bull pen to hold a meeting. Frank couldn't leave without embarrassment, so he sat there and listened to several of the agents talk about their sales. The more they talked, the more discouraged Frank became. They were talking about things he knew he couldn't possibly do.

Then Mr. Talbot made a statement that was to have a profound and lasting effect on Frank Bettger's life. The statement was this. *"This business of selling boils down to one thing. Just one thing. Seeing the people. Show me an individual of ordinary ability who will go out and enthusiastically tell his story to four or five people every day and I'll show you a salesperson who just can't help making good."* That lifted Bettger right out of his chair. He believed anything Mr. Talbot said. Here was an individual with credibility. He had earned it. He had started in the company when he was only 11 years old. He had been on the street selling for years. Mr. Talbot knew what he was talking about.

Frank made up his mind to take Mr. Talbot at his word. He gave himself a pep talk. "You've got two good legs. You can do it. You can tell your story to four or five people every day. You will make good. Why? Mr. Talbot said so." *Bettger said, "What a great relief came over me. Now I knew I was going to make good in selling."*

Putting enthusiasm to work and developing the slight edge became the cornerstones of Frank Bettger's selling career. Many consider him to be the greatest insurance agent ever.

Bettger was a student of self. So are you, or you wouldn't be reading this book. Bettger was willing to learn and change. So are you.

The Slight Edge Creed

I. *Put enthusiasm to work for you.*
II. *Show that you care — by attitude, word and action.*
III. *Treat the customer as you would like to be treated.*
IV. *Respect prospects' intelligence; never overestimate prospects' information.*
V. *Do today's jobs today —never put off until tomorrow.*
VI. *Make right first impressions.*
VII. *Seek an answer to every question; never leave the customer in doubt.*
VIII. *Deliver more than customers expect.*
IX. *Do what it takes to assure the customers' satisfaction.*
X. *Follow-up to make sure the job is well done, and done right.*

Positioning Precept
Develop The Slight Edge

Out-Distance Competition

*Learn from others, strive to be a perfectionist.
Believe in over-compensation. Never follow
the line of least resistance. Practice the
correct way, not the easy way. These
attitudes overcome the opposition
and bring victory.*

-Frank Leahy

A Detroit salesman has a plaque on his office wall that reads: *"My competitors do more for me than my friends do. My friends are too polite to point out my weaknesses, but my competitors go to great expense to advertise them. My competitors are efficient, diligent and attentive. They force me to search for ways to improve my technique and my service. My competitors would take my customers away from me if they could. This keeps me alert to hold what I have. If I had no competitors, I might become complacent and inattentive. I need the discipline they force upon me. I salute my competitors. They have been good to me; God bless them all."*

To out-distance your competition you must learn more and better ways to out-serve them. You then become your own best recommendation.

Stan Gault, Goodyear's CEO, talks about how modern-day sales reps out-distance their competition. *"They always research what prospects say they need, want and expect. They continue the research even when their product is the market leader."*

Demonstrate in every way possible a genuine interest in your prospects, their problems, their concerns and their aspirations. Counsel and assist them in discovering for themselves how your product provides the best solution for their problems and brings within reach the things they want to accomplish.

To out-distance the competition, all you must do is learn to out-serve them. *You do this by consistently doing the right thing in the right way at the right time and always in the best interest of your prospects.*

To gain the reputation of being a master salesperson you must always be a master servant. Study the master doctors of the world, the master lawyers and master accountants. They are master servants and this is true of every relationship of life. You can increase your power to serve, to the satisfaction and profit of both the buyer and you.

Here are three relatively simple strategies which will gain you an edge on the competition in your relationships with prospects and clients.

- **Dress, speak, act and write appropriately**. If suits are ties and preferred at your marketplace, wear them. Speak clearly and stick to the point. Act sharp. Even if you're tired, try to look bright and energetic. You won't win points if prospects perceive you as lazy, or someone who stayed out too late.

- **Never miss an opportunity to do someone a favor**. Chances are it will be returned. But don't keep score — and don't use the favor as "blackmail" to get your prospect to do one for you.

- **Read as much as possible about your field of business**. Broad knowledge about your products and services will lift you head and shoulders above your competitors in the eyes of your prospects, and bring you the success you seek.

The greatest salesperson gave us the secret to mastering competition when He said: *He who would be chief among you must be the servant of all."* And it was said of Him this:

> *"The meek and the gentle*
> *The ribald and the rude*
> *He took them as He found them*
> *And did them all good."*

He out-served his competitors. Follow this perfect example and out-distance your competitors with the same strategy, by out-serving them. Let nothing shake that conviction out of you.

Positioning Precept
Out-Distance Competition

Build Your R & D Department

*It has been said of professional athletes that they
are only as good as their last game. Unless a career
has been completed, yesterday's success may be
lost by today's performance. This, likewise,
applies to all individuals of accomplishment.*

-Frederick Lobl

Periodically you must step back and look at yourself. Are you satisfied with the human being you're becoming? How are you doing in your business? Are you moving forward? Are you getting better? Are your sales increasing? Are you using your time effectively? It's for these reasons you need a personal Research and Development Department.

You must have a library of sales support material you can use and refer to in order to make yourself a better sales rep, to keep you current on your products and to keep you sharp on new selling techniques. There are many services available to keep you up-to-date on product developments and your competition. We recommend you belong to a Book-of-the-Month Club, that you subscribe to Wall Street Journal and good business magazines which keep you up-to-date on current issues. You'll want to subscribe to a good magazine on sales, like *Personal Selling* — and a self-improvement magazine like *Success Unlimited.*

Good sales reps are those who have confidence in themselves and their abilities. *Great sales reps are those whose clients have confidence in them and their abilities.* For this reason, you'll want to develop a Research and Development Department which keeps you abreast. Professionals know they are good, and they know why they are good. Consistently, they work at becoming better.

All of us are aware of tragic school dropouts. But salespeople "drop out," too. It's unfortunate but true that for many there comes a time when they literally "drop out." They stop learning. They stop growing. They stop getting better. It's at this precise point they compromise what they will become as sales reps and as human beings. They expect their companies to grow and get better. *But all too often, sales reps make the assumption that they are good enough to meet the challenge and change of the future without improving themselves.*

Late in the 19th Century, the head of the U.S. Patent Office wanted to slow down his department. And for an interesting reason. He said everything worthwhile had already been invented. Yet each day there are now 300 to 400 hundred patents applied for and there is a waiting list of over 200,000. Can the sales rep of tomorrow hold onto old ways of doing things by saying, "What worked in the past will work in the future?" We don't think so. You must regularly re-evaluate your knowledge and your selling skills.

Remind yourself to keep growing. Keep learning and studying. Keep records to monitor and measure your performance. Maintain a personal Research and Development Department that keeps you up-to-date — one that keeps your sales success "above the crowd" that is not interested in gaining more knowledge and becoming better.

Build a Research and Development Department. Keep it current. *It's an investment which will serve you well.*

Positioning Precept
Build Your R & D Department

Cope With Change

*In the short time between now and the twenty-first century,
millions of capable, psychologically normal people will
face an abrupt collision with the future. Many of them
will find it increasingly painful to keep up with the
incessant demand for change that characterizes
our time. For them, the future will
have arrived too soon.*

-Alvin Toffler

Here is a most interesting study. An economist condensed 50,000 years of recorded history into just 50 years. In this distilled version of history, it was only 10 years ago that you and I emerged from the cave. The first 40 years meant practically nothing in the way of progress. It was just two years ago that Christ walked along the shores of the Sea of Galilee. Gutenberg invented the printing press to make possible the vast communication of today. That was 10 months ago. Ten days ago Edison discovered electricity. It was on that same day that Sheldon fathered salesmanship. Last week, the Wright Brothers made that first successful airplane ride. Five days ago someone pushed a button and you heard your first radio broadcast from KDKA in Pittsburgh. Late yesterday another button was pushed and you viewed television for the first time. It was a matter of minutes ago that the first jet broke the sound barrier. Only a few seconds later, Armstrong landed on the moon.

There is nothing so constant as change. But it's the acceleration of change in this computer age which gives you an idea of the kind of world in which we live and sell in today. And the world in which you'll sell tomorrow. The population is going to double in the next 30 years. With the total fund of knowledge now doubling every three years, the professional salesperson has an opportunity totally unprecedented. How you cope with this opportunity is up to you.

As we pointed out earlier, every salesperson who is conscientious about his or her job understands how important it is to know. You must constantly learn as much as possible about the products and services you sell. Study and carefully examine the sales strategies you use with your prospects. Look for ways in which you can improve your selling skills. Success in selling is determined in large measure by your ability to deal effectively with others. You'll want to consciously add to your understanding of people. Develop an insatiable thirst for knowledge about your products, your procedures and people. Eagerly seek to know in each of these areas.

Next, you must develop the confident feeling that comes from knowing you know. Keep yourself so well-informed that you are completely sold on the value of the job that you're doing for your growing list of customers. *Always be engaged in some type of self-improvement.* This makes you more capable, more self-confident and more in demand.

Finally, become known for what you know. This calls for action. *"Knowledge,"* says Bacon, *"is power".* But here knowledge is not power — it is only possibility. *It becomes power only when put into action!*

Knowledge in action is power. And its highest reward is paid to the professionals in selling who are "on course for tomorrow" and in league with the future. *They know. They know they know. They have become known for what they know.*

Positioning Precept
Cope With Change

Build Your "Replacement Value"

*No one can cheat you out of
ultimate success but yourself.*

-Ralph Waldo Emerson

We've discovered many of the great thoughts on selling originated with our colleague of years past, the incomparable Earl Nightingale. One time in Fort Lauderdale over lunch, Earl steered the discussion to the interesting concept of "replacement value."

"You fellas are engaged in very important work. You're providing a much needed service. Have you ever thought about it?" he asked. *"You're educating salespeople on how they can improve their 'replacement values.' The more indispensable they become, the more difficult they are to replace and the more money they earn."* That's an interesting thought, isn't it? It's one we've never forgotten.

The parking lot attendant can be replaced somewhat easily and quickly. Not so for the heart surgeon — or for you, the effective, professional salesperson. Now who do you suppose has the higher replacement value? Who do you think will earn the greater income? *Income potential is determined by "replacement value."* This helps us understand the wide range of incomes among salespeople. Those who are students of selling and who dedicate themselves to becoming more effective at what they do, become more indispensable. And it's reflected in their paychecks.

Here are 10 practical ways to increase your indispensability.

- **Cultivate a pleasing sales personality and show an ever-improving sales record**. If you can report consistent sales results that wouldn't exist without you — that's the single best form of job insurance we know.

- **Know your merchandise**. Know the outstanding sales points. Justify price by proving quality.

- **"Tune in" to where your customer is**. Acknowledge waiting customers. Be responsive to requests for service.

- **Find out what your customer wants**. Don't jump to conclusions. Ask intelligent, probing questions.

- **Plan your presentations**. If there is a chance, show a variety of merchandise. Display your merchandise effectively. Get agreement from your customers and assist them with their decisions.

- **Increase your average sales (add-on selling).** Make helpful suggestions. Show the merchandise as you suggest it. Suggest larger quantities, better quality, or related items.

- **Learn to cut costs**. Search for ways to reduce expenses. Become known as a cost cutter.

- **Find a profitable niche.** Sell in those areas where you excel. Find a way to do it better than anyone else.

- **Do the mundane.** There are always those territories no one wants. There are products no one wants to handle. Focus on the areas others tend to avoid.

- **Strive for customer satisfaction**. Complete sales promptly and accurately. Thank the customer and ask him or her to return.

Take inventory of where you stand. What's happening to your "replacement value?" Are you doing the things that will make you more indispensable? The answer to these questions is the answer to your current earning potential and your future in sales.

Positioning Precept
Build Your "Replacement Value"

Precept Supporting Philosophies

What we become depends on what we read after all manners of professors have done their best for us. The true university of today is a collection of books.
— Thomas Carlyle

It is one of the paradoxes of success that the things and ways which got you there are seldom those things that keep you there.
— Charles Handy

Most of us plateau when we lose the tension between where we are and where we ought to be.
— John Gardiner

Those that won't be counseled can't be helped.
— Benjamin Franklin

As a rule, those who have the most information will have the greatest success in life.
— Disraeli

A crisis must never be experienced for a second time.
— Peter Drucker

The truly educated have been mentored, either in person or by reading or association, by superior minds with greater skills and mature spirits.
— Fred Smith

Work is dull only to those who take no pride in it.
— William Feather

Off The Professionals' Bookshelf

Ailes, Roger. *You Are The Message.* Doubleday.

Crosby, Philip B. *Quality Is Free.* New American Library, 1980.

Dychtwald, Ph.D., Ken. *Age Wave.* J.P. Tarcher; Martins Press, 1989.

Flesch, Rudolph. *How To Write, Speak and Think More Effectively.* New American Library, 1963.

Funk, Wilfred. *The Way To Vocabulary Power.* Funk, Inc., 1946.

Gardner, John W. *Excellence.* Harper & Row, 1965.

Joneward, Dorothy. *Born To Win.* Addison Wesley.

McFarland, Kenneth. *Eloquence in Public Speaking.* Prentice-Hall, 1959.

Sarnoff, Dorothy. *Speech Can Change Your Life.* Doubleday & Company, 1970.

Yager, Dexter R. *The Business Handbook.* InterNET Services.

Life Style
Disciplines

Stay balanced. Live your life each day as you would climb a mountain. An occasional glance toward the summit keeps the goal in mind, but many beautiful scenes are to be observed from each new vantage point. Climb slowly, steadily, enjoying each passing moment; and the view from the summit will serve as a fitting climax for the journey.

Compete Don't Compare

Some other house, some other car
Than what you drive, or where you are.
We envy other people's faces
Yet before you go trade places
Think, for it's most likely true,
That other people envy you.

-Charles Osgood

The greatest freestyle swimmer of all time, Janet Evans, owns 45
National titles, four gold medals and three world records. Just
before the race for Olympic qualification on the Atlanta Team, her
coach, Mark Schubert, pulled her aside. Coach Schubert said to
her, *"Don't forget who you are."*

At the U.S. Olympic Trials, Evans was surrounded by younger and
perhaps hungrier swimmers. One said she thought the 24-year-old
Evans was scared of the other competition. So as Evans walked to
the starting blocks for the 400-meter freestyle, her coach took just
a moment to remind his swimmer of her credentials. *Don't forget*
who are — compete, but don't compare!

Janet Evans went out and made her third Olympic team, winning
the 400-meter freestyle in splendid fashion.

Janet Evans, with Coach Schubert's help, learned that winning
means excelling at being you. *"You have the right to win, to*
succeed, to make plans, to see those plans fulfilled, to become the
best you can possibly become." Those words were written by
David S. Viscott, M.D.

The former Cleveland Browns' All-Pro, Bill Glass, now a well-known prison evangelist, often says to his huge crusade audiences, *"Be yourself, but learn to be your best self. Don't use being yourself as an excuse for laziness or mediocrity. Be what you ought to be. Stretch toward what you are created to be and in the stretching you're certain to become a better and more effective person."*

Each of us measures success differently. However, we can all agree that success in selling today isn't measured by what we are. It's measured by what we are compared to what we could be. In other words, measure your individual success in selling by comparing it to your real potential — your best self. Coy Eklund, the former Equitable Life, CEO, developed a good thought when he said, *"Most salespeople are presently capable of performing far better than they ever choose to do. They have the skill, the knowledge, the support information and the capacity to do a better job, but the will must accompany the skill. They must have the spirit and be thinking right."*

Thinking right is knowing that whatever it is you want from your sales career — whether it be wealth, expression, excitement, security, travel or leisure, you can get more of it faster by forming the habit of competing with yourself. You'll likely hold yourself to a higher standard than will others.

You will gain the reputation of being a strong competitor by following these five guidelines:

Know thyself. Then you can be true to your best self. Goethe said, *"Before you do something great, you must become something great."*

Believe in self-development. As our good friend and mentor, Fred Smith, puts it, *"There's magic in believing if you don't believe in magic."* All development is self-development.

Be self-disciplined. Put forth honest, intelligent effort. Time invested in this way has its yield. Shallow people believe in luck, but as Emerson said, *"The wise, the strong, the successful people believe in cause and effect."* It's the sure way to achieve excellence. And, do your homework. Have all the facts and the figures ready before plunging into anything. Spectacular results, as we've pointed out previously, always are preceded by unspectacular preparation.

Know the score. Stay informed. Keep the score. Learn from the score. And the score will improve.

Always bounce back. Into each life some rain must fall. Expect it, accept it and forget it. View defeat as a temporary thing. Remember, genius is only the power of making continuous effort. Compete don't compare.

Now, a few years ago the United States Chamber of Commerce reported surveys showed that the working population actually falls into three groups. First, the group that can work but needs close supervision. They comprise 84 percent of all workers. Second, those who can work and manage themselves; they comprise 14 percent. And then there's a third group. They can work, they can manage themselves and in addition, they can plan and create their own work. They represent only two percent. And, of course, they're the most highly paid.

When you made the decision to enter the insurance business, you decided to join the two percent who are expected to plan and create their own work. To do so successfully, you must recognize priorities daily.

We believe that the best kept secret in insurance selling is this: *The degree of an agent's success depends upon his ability to recognize the few priority items that make the difference in consistently achieving superior results.* Those priority items are well worth writing down and remembering. First, plan each day in advance. Secondly, prospect continuously. Third, pre-approach three new people each day. And, fourth, prepare yourself for each interview.

Positioning Precept
Compete Don't Compare

Live On Right Side Of "But"

Life is a matter of development or decay. You either grow or
you retrogress. There's no standing still. You go backward
or forward. The challenge will make you grow, if you are
willing to assert a leadership and look on the challenge
as something to be met and disposed of.

-Everett M. Dirksen

One of the most profitable changes you can discipline yourself to make is to start selling on the right side of the conjunction "but."

When we sell on the wrong side of "but," we have a habit of saying such things as, "Oh, I guess the sales meeting was OK, *but* it was a little long."

We sell on the wrong side of "but" when our attitude causes us to say, "I suppose I do have a great deal to be grateful for, *but* I wish I didn't have all of this follow-up paperwork to complete."

We sell on the wrong side of "but" when we complain, "Sure, I have good products to sell, *but* the competition is awfully keen, and prospects just aren't buying like they should."

Marcus Bach, in *Success Magazine*, writes about his Aunt Selma who lived for many years on the wrong side of "but." When asked if she enjoyed a certain movie, she would respond, "It was good, *but* it should have had a different ending." After she started living on the other side of "but," her answer to the same question became, "It could have a had different ending, but it was wonderful. I enjoyed it!"

When asked how the church service was, Bach's Aunt Selma would answer: "Not too bad, but the songs surely didn't fit the sermon." After she began living on the right side of the conjunction, she would answer, "The songs didn't fit the sermon, but I got some good out of it anyway."

What side of the conjunction "but" are you selling on today? If you sell on the right side of "but," your reactions are positive, affirmative, and optimistic! Your attitude is one of hope, confidence and enthusiasm.

When you comment on a speaker, a program or a sales meeting, you probably state it something like this, "It might have been a bit long, *but* I got several great ideas; the time was well spent."

Because you are a professional salesperson, your conversation takes on an air of expectancy, gratitude and radiance. You are the kind of person who is likely to say: "You're right — things aren't as good as I'd like them to be, but they're not as bad as the others are making them out to be!"

Selling on the right side of "but" causes you to affirm, "Yes, the competition gets tougher, *but* I work for the best company. I sell the best products and it's great to be alive and selling for my company!"

> *The human will, that force unseen,*
> *The offspring of a deathless soul*
> *Can wind its way to any goal*
> *Though walls of granite intervene.*

James Allen

Positioning Precept
Live On Right Side Of "But"

Develop What It Takes

It's what we do regularly — everyday, without
fail — that determines what we gain or lose.
If one really dedicates time and talents to
the objective of personal improvement
each hour and day, then one's life
will be in good hands.

-Coy Eklund

"They've got what it takes!"

How often have you heard successful performers described that way? How many times do you suppose that observation is being made by individuals who have not bothered to take the time to study "What It Takes" to be ranked as a star in selling?

Think of the exceptionally successful salespeople you know. You'll discover, as we have, they possess most, if not all of these seven characteristics:

- **Intensely Goal-Oriented** - Some call it vision. Others describe it as purpose, a definite chief aim or a mission statement. Regardless of what you call it, it's important to have a thought-out dream reduced to writing. *Building your dream carefully brings the future into the present so you can do something about it now.*

- **High Level of Energy** - Most refer to this as the foundation of their competitive edge. They can start earlier and stay later than the competition.

- **Mastery of Sales Lines** - They are over-rehearsed. Consequently, they feel in control. The words they use are expressed as naturally as they breathe.

- **Do not take "no" personally and allow it to make them feel inferior** - They have high enough levels of confidence or self-esteem so that, although they may be disappointed, they are not devastated.

- **Impeccably honest with self and customers** - No matter what the temptation to short-cut might be, these people resisted and gained ongoing trust of customers.

- **High levels of empathy** - The ability to put themselves in their prospects' shoes, imagine needs and respond appropriately. They make their recommendation their prospects' idea. They are in agreement with Pascal who said, *"People are generally better persuaded by the reasons which they have themselves discovered than by those which have come into the minds of others."*

- **100% Accountable** - Successful sales reps don't blame the economy, the competition, or their company for dips in sales. Instead, the poorer things become, the harder they worked to turn things around.

How do you measure up? What should you be doing to develop what it takes? Selling is a great field filled with opportunity. But that opportunity must be utilized. *This takes study, concentration and focus.*

The well-known dentist, Dr. David Hildebrand, has a philosophy on his desk. It has always made a lot of sense to us. This is what it says: *"God doesn't waste time making a nobody. It's up to us to*

develop our God-given talents as He commands us to do.''
Go back and review the seven traits again. You'll discover they
are controllable. *You can have what it takes!*

Positioning Precept
Develop What It Takes

Enrich Your Mind

People can't become truly knowledgeable without being excellent readers. While multimedia systems can use video and sound to deliver information in compelling ways, text is still one of the best way to convey details.

-Bill Gates

Here are four success-proven guideposts. They will lead you to greater achievements. They will enrich your mind.

- **Read.** *"Resolve to edge in a little reading every day,"* Horace Mann advised, *"even if it is but a single paragraph or two. If you invest in reading only 15 minutes a day, it will make itself felt by the end of the year."*

  Setting aside just 15 minutes a day will enable you to read by up to two dozen books a year. Keep it up and you'll have read 1,000 books in your lifetime. *That's the equivalent of going through college five times.*

  Earl Nightingale once wrote, *"Books have meant to my life what the sun has meant to the planet earth."*

- **Mark.** The books we cherish most — the ones which become our closest friends — are well marked. Their sentences and paragraphs are underlined in red, in blue, in green, and in yellow. *To get the most from your books and periodicals, form the habit of reading with a pen or highlighter in hand.* The riches of reading will rapidly multiply for you as you mark, underline, challenge, and often editorialize in the margins. We find ourselves jotting cross-index information in the margins; e.g., "See

Mackay's chapter on this subject." Such notations are quite valuable when preparing speeches or presentations on rather short notice.

- **Learn.** To learn is to understand, to comprehend, or to attain proficiency in a subject. One of the most effective ways of learning is to outline the book. Incidentally, these same book outlines make great enclosures for letters going to prospects and clients.

- **Inwardly Digest.** It's not only what individuals eat, but also what they digest, that gives them strength. *Likewise, it's not only what we read and how much we read, but what we "digest," what we "internalize" that adds to our knowledge and understanding.*

Digesting food involves the breaking down and relating to existing forces in the stomach and intestines. Digesting reading material involves a similar type of action — relating to knowledge, attitudes and experiences which are already a part of our personalities.

To inwardly digest the reading you do is an essential part of the reading process, if you want your reading to give you the most in mental pleasure, intellectual growth and professional inspiration.

Bishop Fulton J. Sheen emphasized the value of having sufficient "mental juices" to help in the digestion of what we read. He warned, *"As the stomach can suffer from indigestion, so can the mind. If too many ideas are poured into it and there are not sufficient juices of the intellect to absorb them, a queer kind of literary constipation follows."*

This inscription for the Children's Reading Room, Hopkinton, Massachusetts, might well be placed in your study:

> *"Books are keys to wisdom's treasure;*
> *Books are gates to lands of pleasure;*
> *Books are paths that upward lead;*
> *Books are friends, come let us read."*

Learn the riches of reading. It will enrich your mind — and improve your sales!

Positioning Precept
Enrich Your Mind

Build Goodwill

In selling, as in business and politics, you will need a lot of people, spread out in the right places, whom you can depend upon — because they can depend on you.

-Michael Korda

Building a professional image tends to soften your market. It facilitates the process of turning prospects into customers. It keeps these customers coming back and endorsing you to others. Building a professional image brings profitable growth to your business or practice.

These are seven ways in which you can build your image:

1)   **Project Success** - Prospects focus on *you* before they focus on what you are selling. Their perception of you carries considerable influence in their decision to do business with you. The way you look and behave says things to prospects and clients. It tells them whether you are a seasoned professional or an amateur. Study successful salespeople. Observe the types of appearance and behavior they exhibit. Cultivate an appearance that projects an image of competence, confidence, and pride in your sales performance. *A good rule to follow is to always look as if you care how you look.*

2)   **Project Professionalism** - When prospects and clients come into your office, they expect to see professionalism. *Make certain they see and feel evidence of success.* They should be greeted warmly and made to feel welcome. In addition to attractive and appropriate artwork, they should see your professional designations on your office wall.

3) **Project Good Taste** - Carefully consider the design of business cards and stationery you use. Keep both conservative. Make sure the title you use reflects what you do. An attractive brochure can enhance your image. It can display your credentials and communicate to your prospects the broad range of products and services you sell.

4) **Establish A Network** - This is not something you do overnight. It takes years of networking. These are relationships you build with people you can rely upon. These are colleagues for whom you do favors. You support their projects. You listen to their problems and they do the same for you.

5) **Project a Message** - Regular, informative mailings to key customers and prospects keep your name in circulation, in mind. It does this in an inexpensive, positive, non threatening way. You will want to investigate the several industry-related newsletters that can be sent monthly or quarterly.

6) **Target Advertising** - When you advertise in professional journals and newsletters, you can build your image with certain target groups. Advertising is expensive. The results are generally hard to measure. You'll want to use it only when the publication targets the audience you are trying to reach.

7) **Write Articles and Schedule Speaking Engagements** - An excellent strategy to help you become known for what you know is to publish articles. Trade-association journals and newsletters are usually looking for articles. Published material establishes you as an authority. Circulating re-prints will have a powerful influence on prospects and clients. Use industry, club, and community speaking engagements to build your image in front of potential

customers. These organizations are usually looking for speakers. As with written articles, speeches create a powerful image of you as an authority.

Positioning Precept
Build Goodwill

Know What Is Important

*The greatest satisfaction in the world
is work well done.*

-J. C. Penney

It's been said we don't need education so much as we need re-minding. We're not sure that's exactly true, but in sales it is good to remind ourselves from time to time just what's important.

The late Earl Nightingale, our teacher, mentor and colleague, sent us some definitions one time called *The Greatest Things.* During our sales careers, we've reviewed them often to help us remember just what's important and what isn't.

Here they are — *The Greatest Things:*

The best day, today.
The greatest puzzle, life.
The best policy, honesty.
The greatest thought, God.
The greatest mystery, death.
The best work, work you like.
The greatest mistake, giving up.
The most ridiculous asset, pride.
The greatest need, common sense.
The most dangerous person, a liar.
The best advice, use good manners.
The wisest short-cut, develop mentors.
The greatest fault, to be aware of none.
The greatest truth, we reap what we sow.
The most expensive indulgence, self-pity.
The greatest deceiver, one who deceives self.
The best habit, making good on all commitments.

The best teacher, one who brings out the best in you.
The saddest feeling - feeling envious of another's success.
The worse bankruptcy, the salesperson without enthusiasm.
The greatest thing in the world, love — love of family, home, friends, associates, company and country.

And here are some definitions taken from the back of business cards and meeting notes we've accumulated along the way. They are from some of the top salespeople in the world.
The greatest handicap, egotism.
The greatest victory, victory over self.
The most certain thing in business, change.
The greatest job, being needed and appreciated.
The greatest gamble, substituting hope for facts.
The strongest competitive edge, a high level of energy.
The most effective selling habit, sound time management.
The greatest guarantee of success, honest intelligent effort.
The most expensive indulgence, poor money management.
The best action, keeping the mind clear and judgment good.
The greatest selling strategy, speaking as one who has authority.

The greatest waste, the vast reservoir of talents and abilities most of us possess but never quite get around to using.

And again, the greatest three-word strategy of all ...

... "And Then Some"

These three little words can sweep you to greatness in selling. They are the difference between average salespeople and top salespeople.

The high achievers always do what is expected ... *and then some.* They hold themselves responsible for higher standards. They make good on commitments and responsibilities ... *and then some.*

They can be counted on to represent themselves and their companies in a professional manner. Their spirit of service is summed up in these little words ... *and then some!*

Positioning Precept
Know What Is Important

Live Within Income

Somewhere along the line, the lack of good financial
management becomes a barrier to professional growth,
no matter how talented the salesperson. It eats into
concentration and confidence.

-Dan Sullivan

At any given time, you can measure what kind of shape you're in
by responding to three simple questions:

- *Do you earn more than you spend?* If you don't spend
  less than you earn, you don't have a place to start.
  You're a disaster waiting to happen.
- *Are you prudent by reducing your debt load?* Do you
  owe less money at the end of the year than you owed at
  the beginning?
- *Are you an active saver and investor?* Have you
  accumulated enough for your age and income? Study
  after study on retirement planning shows the same
  thing. People are not saving enough. Merrill Lynch
  says baby boomers are saving a third of what they will
  need. A CNN/Gallop Poll shows 40 percent of
  boomers saved less than $1,000 last year.

Why do we refer to those individuals who plan and manage their
finances as "four percenters?" *It's because only four percent of the*
population can be considered financially successful at age 65.
Statistics from the U.S. Department of Health and Human Services
(SSA PUB #13-11871, 6/90) demonstrate that for every 100 people
beginning their careers at age 25, the following situations exist at
age 65:

- 25 will be dead.
- 20 will have annual incomes under $6,000.
- 51 will have annual incomes between $6,000 and $35,000.
- *Four will have an annual income of more than $35,000.*

You can decide now to be among the "four percenters" who achieve financial success. *You are today the consequence of all the decisions you've made in the past. Since that's true, you can be the cause of your own future.* The decisions you make today will determine what your tomorrows will be like.

Think of the words of Ralph Waldo Emerson, *"Shallow people believe in luck; they believe in circumstances. Strong people believe in cause and effect."* By making a financial plan, you are putting cause and effect on your side. *You are becoming pro-active in managing your finances.*

The "minority" who achieve financial success share three traits: **First, "four percenters" pursue specific goals and objectives**. It's not enough for you to dream of building your own house, buying an expensive car, taking your family on a once-in-a-life-time vacation, sending your children to college or enjoying a comfortable retirement. Unless you write down your dreams in specific terms and begin to take action to achieve them, the chances are good you'll never see them come true.

It's encouraging to know that people who write down their personal goals achieve, on the average, 96 percent of what they list. It's also sobering to realize that less than seven percent of the population takes the time to write out their goals.

Second, the "four percenters" are serious about planning. Notice carefully the words of Bernard Baruch, the one-time, internationally known financier. He wrote: *"The success or failure of a long range savings and investment plan is not predicated on the rate of return. Its success depends on the use of a systematic plan of putting money in and leaving it there."*

Unfortunately, most individuals are causal about their own money. They put a small amount in a savings account. Perhaps they buy a few stocks and bonds. They buy a house and some furniture, but they don't actually plan. Usually they spend their income on a needs basis. It's not until one of the children wants to go to college, a member of the family becomes ill or the principal wage earner reaches retirement that they are confronted with the profound importance of financial planning. *The average American family spends more time discussing their yearly vacation than their financial future!*

Third, "four percenters" have control over their lives. When you've written your goals and formulated a plan, the challenge has only begun. Unfortunately, most people — even those with goals and plans — don't follow consistent practices when making financial decisions. Rather, they react to day-to-day pressures and emotional desires.

With specific goals and a financial plan, you'll be in a position to make rational, proactive financial decisions. *One of the traits that made you successful in your career can undermine you financially. This trait is optimism. Successful salespeople are almost always optimistic and usually, a bit naive.* The happiest, most well adjusted and productive individuals believe the best is about to happen. They see the future as bright and full of promise. They feel good about tomorrow.

Here's the drawback to that positive attitude from an economic perspective: *Typically, optimistic and maybe a bit naive, individuals do not plan for emergencies.* They enlarge the office, purchase sophisticated equipment, hire extra personnel or buy new furniture on the assumption that the business revenues will be there by the time the bills come due. *A recent study indicated the typical American buys $1,300 on credit for every $1,000 he or she earns! By contrast, "four percenters" have the self-control necessary to balance their optimism in money matters with disciplined spending. They use their financial goals and budget to determine what they'll do and when they'll do it.*

Self-control is vital to you, because in selling, your income is seldom level throughout the year. You need a plan which allows you to manage the periods of high revenue so that when your income is at its low point, you'll still be able to fulfill your obligations. Your plan should take into consideration these 10 recommendations:

- *Develop a business budget as well as a personal budget.*

- *Save 10 percent of your net business income. We cannot overemphasize the importance of this one.*

- *Think, talk and plan in terms of "net business income."*

- *Decide to invest at least 20 percent back into your business.*

- *Give 10 percent of your income to your church, synagogue or favorite charity.*

- *Read and inwardly digest books on money management.*

- *Become knowledgeable on investing, respecting your need to balance risk/reward.*

- *Have one credit card only.*

- *Choose a competent tax professional and work closely with him or her.*

- *Review your results monthly.*

Your financial fitness is ultimately a reflection of the choices you make, one-by-one, day-by-day.

Positioning Precept
Live Within Income

Extend Your Stay

Everyone needs at least three ingredients
for a successful life – a self fit to live with,
a faith fit to live by, and a work fit to live for.

-Dr. George Sweeting

"How can I feel better and extend my stay on earth longer?"
That's one of the questions most often asked by professionals
searching for a fool-proof prescription.

Time Magazine carried an article by Dr. George W. Comstock of
Johns Hopkins School of Hygiene and Public Health. Here is what
he had to say. *"Nice guys do literally finish last."* In studies of
the relation of social economic factors to disease and the population of Washington County, Maryland, Comstock and his colleagues made an incidental but fascinating discovery. Regular
church-going, and the clean living that often goes with it, appear to
help people avoid a whole bagful of dire ailments and disasters -
among them, heart disease, cirrhosis of the liver, tuberculosis,
cancer of the cervix, chronic bronchitis, fatal one-car accidents and
suicide. In addition, the average church-goer lives 5.7 years longer
than the average non church-goer.

The famed Cooper Aerobic Clinic in Dallas has attracted more
than 60,000 individuals — presidents, professional athletes, corporate executives, leaders from all walks of life since Dr. Kenneth
Cooper started the clinic. Though they come with every ailment
known to medical science, what they really want to know is *"How
can I feel better, have more energy and extend my stay on earth?"*

What does Dr. Cooper say to them? Well, one time we heard him
say, *"Many individuals today do not die — they kill themselves."*

In other words, Dr. Cooper believes a large number of the clinic's patients could have prevented their own illnesses or early deaths.

According to the experts, there are seven steps to take if you wish to extend your stay and live longer, healthier days on earth.

- **Stay Active.** Once considered an indulgence for a few, regular exercise is now a must for all. *"Moderate exercise seems to be enough to make you healthy - only 30 minutes of walking once a day,"* according to Dr. Dean Ornish, well known for his program for reversing heart disease. *"It may be a mistake to exercise more than 30 minutes a day just to live longer. If you choose to do more, then you do it because you enjoy it, not just to live longer,"* suggests Dr. Ornish. You don't have to suffer to feel good. *Make exercise a "playout" instead of a workout.*

  By exercising regularly you can do more gradually, greatly benefiting your cardiovascular system, energy level and mental alertness. But don't just create your own exercise program. Ask your doctor to recommend one that's best suited for you.

- **Be Optimistic.** Physiologically, happiness is a state of mind which is healthy for the body. Depressed individuals suffer a slowing down of the metabolic processes. A merry heart does good like medicine, says the proverb, but a broken heart dries the bones.

  "You can will yourself to be ill," says Dr. Albert Hagedorn, a Mayo Clinic section head in internal medicine. "A case of nerves is not just 'in your head,' but is as real as a heart attack." The nervous system has a job, like the heart, and its functioning is affected by stress, such as extra responsibility, work or lack of stress management.

"Our patients have similar problems," says Dr. Hagedorn. *"Yet we see many of them die young because they lack a positive attitude."*

An optimistic outlook on things will help you make sales, win customer cooperation, gain support from people closest to you — in short, succeed in life and living.

- **Cope With Adversity.** Victor Frankl, the world-renowned Australian psychiatrist, wrote a remarkable book, *Man's Search For Meaning*. In this book, Frankl describes, in meticulous detail, the trauma and suffering he endured during his incarceration by the Nazis.

  Frankl makes it clear that attitude was an essential, shared element among the survivors. *"Everything can be taken from an individual but one thing - the last of the human freedoms — to choose one's attitude in any given set of circumstances."*

  Adversity, problems, bad things happening are an integral ongoing part of living. If you see the bad things that happen as totally unexpected occurrences, it's easy to sell yourself into believing you are the victim of bad breaks. It's far better to accept the reality that "into each life some rain will fall." Life will be full of difficulties and dilemmas. Accept this reality and you'll be able to focus your energies on coping with adversities as quickly and easily as possible.

  You have little or no control over what happens to you. You have complete control over your reaction. It's all a matter of attitude.

- **Reduce Your Weight.** Many believe it's normal to gain weight as they grow older. This can be a dangerous misconception. *As we age, we gain fat at the expense of muscle.*

Remember, fat people usually don't grow old.

- **Plan Significant Events.** There's nothing more therapeutic than the pursuit of meaningful goals. *Studies made of centenarians, those reaching age 100 and beyond, show they have one theme in common.* They have something significant yet to be done. They have something to look forward to — a motivation for living.

- **Change The Pace.** Get away from your demanding sales work routine and do something you enjoy. *Relief from the day-to-day strains restores the joy of living.*

- **Have Periodic Check-ups.** This is an all important first investment in future good health. This is where preventive action begins.

  It's especially crucial in the age group from 40 to 55, where today's killers creep in.

  If you weather this critical age span and continue to take care of yourself, there's a good chance you'll extend your stay into your 80s and beyond.

Realize a longer, productive life is mostly up to you. More than ever before, longevity is up to the individual. The enormous gain in life expectancy - 76 years in 1995, an increase of nine years since 1940 - is a gift of modern medicine, research and public health measures. *Yet, alert, health-conscious individuals can do more than their doctors to protect themselves.* Knowing this gives you the incentive to be less fatalistic - and to take better care of yourself.

Robust health and a high level of energy — keys to looking and feeling years younger - requires more than following a set of rules. It also involves an optimistic, positive state of mind. Scientists are increasingly proving celebrated pianist Arthur Rubinstein was right when he said, *"I have found if you love life, life will love you back."* Rubinstein lived to be 95.

Positioning Precept
Extend Your Stay

Live In Balance

Successful individuals many times fail in life for reasons which have nothing to do with how they perform in their jobs.

-Dr. George W. Crane

Dr. Thomas Tewell, the widely acclaimed preacher at The Fifth Avenue Presbyterian Church in New York City, relates the sad account of Kim Zmeiskal's quest for the gold medal.

> *It was the women's gymnastics finals in the 1992 Olympics in Barcelona, Spain. Kim Zmeiskal, the slight 4'5" power-horse of an Olympic gymnast who at that time was the world champion, was heavily favored to win the gold medal.*
>
> *Kim mounted the balance beam and for a moment her routine, which had been choreographed, or-chestrated and practiced for hours was absolutely brilliant. She danced across the balance beam! As she did a flip in mid-air, the judges were smiling as they could see she was poised and seemed destined for greatness. Then in that moment the unthinkable happened. Kim Zmeiskal lost her balance. Her coach Bela Karoli along with the crowd gasped, as she not only lost her balance, but fell off the beam. Her hopes for a gold medal and a perfect ten were dashed.*

Like Kim Zmeiskal, many talented salespeople — potential "per-fect ten" performers — lose their balance and with it their effec-tiveness.

Some years ago, Dr. George W. Crane, a professor at Northwestern University, developed the concept that each person carries throughout his and her career a "Cross of Life."* *This cross has five dimensions — professional, physical, financial, personal, and spiritual. When these elements are in balance, a person can function at full capacity.* Dr. Crane feels that far too many people manage to fail for reasons that have nothing to do with the way they perform their jobs. He said, *"They simply get their 'Cross of Life' out of balance."*

Let's examine each dimension of the "Cross" so you can determine for yourself the kinds of habits you want to be developing.

- **Professional Growth** - It's impossible to put a price tag on professional competence, because the payoff for it is far more than extra dollars earned. *It involves such intangibles as personal satisfaction, enjoyment of your work, and stature as a person.*

  Economist John W. Galbraith was asked the secret for consistently achieving excellence in your job. He said, *"Whatever it is you do today, do it better tomorrow."*

- **Physical Self** - The old saying, "If I'd known I was going to live so long, I would have taken better care of myself," is worth considering. People are living longer these days. The Bureau of Census predicts that by the year 2000 about one hundred thousand will be age 100 or older. By 2050, there will be about one million centenarians.

  If you plan to live a long and productive life, taking good care of yourself is very important. The work of a salesperson can be fulfilling, enjoyable, and productive at any age if you take good care of your health and stay active.

- **Financial Well-being** - This third dimension of the "Cross of Life," the condition of your financial balance sheet, is generally a reliable measurement of the balance you are achieving in your life.

  Every salesperson has the right to decide what kind of person he or she will become. You determine what income level you wish to attain, and what you would like your net worth to be. This is your career and yours alone. But never be satisfied with a personal "balance sheet" that is anything less that you want it to be.

- **Personal Life** - For most, this means the "quality time" spent with the members of one's family. As a sales rep, you're sure to discover the difficulty of scheduling such time with them. You can't separate family plans from your personal career development. Discuss your business and your goals with your family. Talk freely about your accomplishments and demonstrate a positive attitude toward your selling job and its future.

- **Spiritual** - Dr. Crane suggests that today most readers and students are searching for the "quick fix" — the mini-course, so to speak. He says it's this final dimension of "The Cross" that makes possible a "quick and reliable" way to achieve balance. The spiritual element provides a strong foundation for stability and purpose in both your professional and personal life. And this spiritual aspect touches and binds together each of the other dimensions. A spiritual element that is really a part of you will enable you to live a harmonious life. Spiritual harmony will keep you well. It will fill you with strength, vitality, and optimism.

Thomas Carlyle said, *"It's the spiritual which always determines the material."* This is one reason for focusing on the spiritual and growing in this important area. The spiritual can and will affect every other area of your personal and professional life in a very positive way.

Again, be reminded Carlyle said: *"There's one life - just a little gleam of time between two vast eternities. No second chance for us, forever more."*

That's reason enough to live in balance, isn't it?

Positioning Precept
Live In Balance

* The "Cross of Life" has an interesting history behind it. The Kinders credit Dr. Crane, the Northwestern University psychology professor, with the concept. However, Dr. Crane was probably introduced to the Cross by Dr. William Kepler of the Mayo Clinic, who in turn learned it from Dr. High Cabot, another prominent Mayo physician, the older brother of Richard Cabot.

Finish Strong

Life is God's gift to us.
What we do with it is our gift to God.

-Horace Mann

On New Year's Day, 1919, Georgia Tech played the University of California in the Rose Bowl. Shortly before half-time, a player named Roy Riegels recovered a fumble for California. Somehow, he got spun around as he headed for the goal line. Roy ran well. He ran fast. But Roy Riegels also ran in the wrong direction. A teammate tackled him just before Roy would have scored for Georgia Tech. When California attempted to punt, Georgia Tech blocked the kick and scored a safety.

California headed off the field and into the locker room. As they sat on the benches, Riegels put a blanket around his shoulders, put his face in his hands, and cried like a baby.

Coach Nibbs Price said nothing. No doubt he was trying to decide what he might do with Riegels. The stunned California players just sat there. When the timekeeper announced the three minute warning, Coach Price looked at the team and said simply, *"The same team that played the first half will start the second."*

All the players got up and started out, except for Riegels. The coach called to him again, but still he didn't move. So he went over to Riegels and said, *"Roy, didn't you hear me? The same team starts the second half!"*

Riegels looked up, with tears in his eyes and said, *"Coach, I can't do it! I've ruined you! I've let down my teammates. I've ruined myself. I can't face the crowd out there in the stadium."* Coach

Price reached out and put his hand on Riegel's shoulder and said, *"Roy, get up and go back. The game is only half over!"*

Roy Riegels went back. Everyone who saw that famous game said it was perhaps the greatest half of football a player ever played. *Riegels brought California back to a strong victory. Roy Riegels finished strong!*

In selling, we often "take the ball and run in the wrong direction." We stumble and fumble and get discouraged with our results. We never want to try again. It's then we must be reminded that most selling hours produce little in the way of results. *Our job is to hang in there and finish strong.*

Over the years, we've discovered those individuals who finish strong have these characteristics:

- *They dream the big dreams. There's nothing in little plans that stirs the blood.*
- *They are practical and realistic.*
- *They think greatly of their function. They fall in love with their work.*
- *They are appearance conscious. They look like winners.*
- *They believe in preparation. They understand that chance favors the prepared, orderly mind.*
- *They like to be effective.*
- *They make responsible commitments.*
- *They respond to responsibility.*
- *They enjoy improving things.*
- *They bounce back!*

We've always liked this thought developed by Peter Drucker: *"It is the spirit that motivates, that calls upon our reserves of dedication and effort, that decides whether we will give our best, finish strong, or just do enough to get by."*

Stick to the task —
      Until it sticks to you.
Beginners are many
      Enders are few.
Honor, power, position and praise
      Comes to those who stick and stay.

Yes, stick to the task
      until it sticks to you.
Bend at it. Sweat it. Smile at it, too.
For out of the bend, the sweat, the smile
      will come life's victories ... in a while.

Positioning Precept
Finish Strong

Precept Supporting Philosophies

Becoming everything one is capable of becoming is the ultimate end of life.
> — Robert Louis Stevenson

Whatever your hand finds to do, do it with all your might.
> — Solomon

The most pathetic person in the world is someone who has sight but no vision.
> — Helen Keller

In making our decisions, we must use the brains that God has given us. But we must also use our hearts which He also gave us.
> — Fulton Oursler

We have very few inferior people in the world. We have lots of inferior environments. Try to enrich your environment.
> — Frank Lloyd Wright

Keeping busy and making optimism a way of life can restore your faith in yourself .
> — Lucille Ball

Getting older may be inevitable, but being old isn't.
> — George Burns

Life is no brief candle to me. It's a sort of splendid torch which I've got hold of for the moment. I want to make it burn as brightly as possible before handing it on to future generations.
> — George Bernard Shaw

Today, nothing is like it was; tomorrow, nothing will be like it is.
> — Dr. Gerald Sentell

Off The Professionals' Bookshelf

Bennett, William J. *The Book of Virtues.* Simon & Schuster, 1993.

Cooper, MD, Kenneth. *It's Better To Believe.* Thomas Nelson, Inc., 1995.

Engstrom, Ted W. *The Pursuit of Excellence.* Zondervan.

Gallup, Jr., George. *The Great American Success Story.* Dow Jones-Irwin, 1986.

Glass, Bill. *How To Win When The Roof Caves In.* Fleming H. Revell.

Minirth, Frank B. and Paul D. Meier. *Happiness Is A Choice.* Baker Bookhouse, 1978.

Myers, Ph.D., David G. *The Pursuit of Happiness.* Morrow & Company.

Naisbitt, John and Pat Aburdene. *Megatrends 2000.* Morrow & Company, 1991.

Sullivan, Dan. *The 21st Century Agent.* The Strategic Coach.

Sweeting, Dr. George. *Secrets of Excellence.* Moody Press, 1985.

Tuma, Jerry and Ramona and Tim LaHaye. *Smart Money.* Multnomah Brooks.

Where Will You Go From Here?

Life seems to be a
       superbly orchestrated play.
There is the grand opening scene,
       the intriguing climax, and
       the inevitable final curtain.
You are free to choose
       a leading role, one of
       the many supporting roles,
       a walk-on or merely
       a prop.
It's all up to you.

Curtain Going Up!

Index

"Jack and Garry Kinder have done it again. *21st Century Positioning* is their seventh book, and proof that seven is indeed the number of perfection. Profitable and productive for every area of life. Read it and reap!"
Dr. 0. S. Hawkins
Pastor, First Baptist, Dallas, TX

"An absolute masterpiece! The finest book on successful selling - and living - ever written."
B. Lee Harrison, Jr., CLU
North Florida Financial Corporation

"This book will position you for the 21st Century with proven, practical 'how to' procedures for selling professionally. It will work wonders for your bank account."
Dr. John Maxwell
Author and Speaker

"To read and listen to Jack and Garry Kinder is like watching and hearing a freight train coming down the track. The closer their concepts get to you, the more they inspire your spirit to become a loud voice in your future.
Read, enjoy, and keep selling."
Thomas J. Berthel
CEO, Berthel Fisher & Company

"From my collegiate and professional football coaches - Joe Paterno, Don Shula, Tom Landry, Marv Levy - I learned how dedication, planning and execution translate into success. The Kinders have been my coaches in business. They have helped me apply the principles I learned from the gridiron to the boardroom."
Charles J. Zapiec, CLU, ChFC, CFP
President & CEO, Sage Financial Advisors

"We've benefited from the Kinders' platform skills and selling precepts for more than 20 years. This is their best stuff. Easy to read and apply."

Dick and Jinger Heath

Founders, BeautiControl

"What an inspiring book for sales professionals! *21st Century Positioning* is bound to become the favorite book for many salespeople. It will help them avoid slumps, keep focused and move forward."

Tom Hopkins

Author, *How to Master the Art of Selling*

"Jack and Garry Kinder have given in-depth sales training to more salespeople than any trainers I have ever met. They are out in the field almost every day. There is no one more qualified to share positioning precepts than the Kinder Brothers."

Vic Conant

President, Nightingale/Conant

"Be careful - This book will take away all excuses for not being immensely successful."

Bob Burg

Author, *Endless Referrals*

"Jack and Garry Kinder brilliantly steer the entrepreneur through the free enterprise system, charting the course from their immense wealth of selling and consulting experience."

Roger Staubach

Chairman & CEO, The Staubach Company

"The Kinder Precepts have helped us to be number one
in golf shop merchandising in Texas for ten years.
They will do the same for you."
Eldridge Miles
Director of Golf, Gleneagles Country Club

"What a great harvest of success precepts to change your life!"
Og Mandino
Author/Speaker

"When Jack and Garry Kinder speak, I listen.
When they write, I read. Everyone who wants to sell and
live more productively should grab *21st Century Positioning,*
the latest and best from the Kinders' powerful pens."
Bob Briner
Author, *Squeeze Play*

"Pure nuggets-bountiful, plentiful, incredible
nuggets of gold on each and every page.
A wonderful and profitable read from two of the masters."
Carl Sewell
Author, *Customers For Life*

"Jack and Garry Kinder have colorfully captured the passion
of selling. The masterful use of illustrations and real-life
events holds your attention, while the depth of the
information and advice point you toward the top."
Mary Kay Ash
Founder & Chairman Emeritus, Mary Kay, Inc.

"This book is a culmination of all the Kinder wisdom and
experience in one package. It carries the impact of Peale's
Power of Positive Thinking and Hill's *Think and Grow Rich.*"
Bob Richards
Motivational Speaker